The
World's
Greatest
Christmas
Activity Book

For
Kids

The World's Greatest Christmas Activity Book

For Kids

KEN SAVE

SHILOH kidz
An Imprint of Barbour Publishing, Inc.

Published by Shiloh Kidz, an imprint of Barbour Publishing, Inc., 1810 Barbour Drive, Uhrichsville, Ohio 44683, www.shilohkidz.com

Our mission is to inspire the world with the life-changing message of the Bible.

 Member of the
Evangelical Christian
Publishers Association

Printed in the United States of America.
06191 0818 BP

THE PICTURES ARE YOUR CLUES. USE THE CIRCLED LETTERS TO
COMPLETE THE PUZZLE BELOW.

THEY WILL BE THE PARENTS OF JESUS. WHO ARE THEY?

FIND THE FOUR

COMPLETE THE PUZZLE BELOW BY CROSSING OUT EVERY LETTER THAT APPEARS AT LEAST FOUR TIMES. USE THE REMAINING LETTERS TO COMPLETE THE SENTENCE.

B	J	C	T	C	T	S	I	W	Y	N
N	X	O	W	C	P	D	X	H	L	Z
J	■	L	R	K	U	P	N	V	V	B
P	I	Q	D	W	B	K	G	E	I	J
D	Q	O	H	■	M	I	S	Z	R	Q
S	G	A	E	V	O	Q	L	K	F	U
G	U	S	P	F	J	N	F	■	■	T
Z	K	Z	E	H	W	X	F	■	C	D
E	V	L	U	H	B	G	T	■	O	X

MARY AND JOSEPH PLAN TO __ __ __ __ __ .

6

DON'T LEAVE IT SCRAMBLED!

UNSCRAMBLE EACH WORD, THEN USE THE CIRCLED LETTERS TO COMPLETE THE PUZZLE BELOW . . . AND I HOPE IT DOESN'T HURT YOUR EYES!

"NI   HET   TXHSI   OHNMT,   DGO

__ ___O___ ___ _____, ___

TSNE   ETH   EALGN   IAGBLER

____ ___ _____ _O_____

OT   RZHTENAA,   A   ONWT   NI

__ _____O___, _ ____ __

EALLGIE,   OT   A   NGIIVR

__O_____, __ _ ___O__

PDGELDE   OT   EB   DMRAIRE

_____O__ __ __ _____

OT   A   ANM   DMNEA   HJSEPO,

__ _ ___ ___O_ _____,

A   NCETDEASDN   FO   DVDIA."

_ _____ __ _____."

LUKE 1:26–27

WHO IS THIS VISITOR?

7

WHERE ARE THOSE VOWELS?

YOU'RE GOING TO HAVE TO CONCENTRATE FOR THIS ONE! VOWELS ARE HIDDEN IN THE PICTURE BELOW. YOU WILL NEED THEM TO COMPLETE THE PUZZLE.

"TH_ _NG_L W_NT T_ H_R _ND

S_ _ _D, 'GR_ _ _T_NGS, Y_ _ WH_ _R_

H_GHLY F_V_R_D! TH_ L_RD _S

W_TH Y_ _ _.'"

LUKE 1:28

8

LETTER CLUES

TO DECODE THIS MESSAGE FROM GOD, YOU'LL NEED TO TAKE THE LETTER FROM EACH NUMBERED CLUE AND MATCH IT TO THE NUMBERED SPACE IN THE PUZZLE BELOW.

1. LOOK FOR THIS IN BOTH *RAFT* AND *HORSE*.

   _____

2. THIS ONE IS SEEN ONCE IN *RUG* AND TWICE IN *JUGGLE*.

   _____

3. THIS LETTER IS FOUND TWICE IN *NONE* AND *NUN*.

   _____

4. BEGINS THE WORD *HOT* AND ENDS THE WORD *TOUGH*.

   _____

5. BEGINS THE WORD *OPEN* AND FOUND SECOND IN *ROPE*.

   _____

6. THIS LETTER IS FOUND ONCE IN *YELLOW* AND *BABY*.

   _____

7. THIS LETTER CAN BE FOUND IN *WHEEL* AND *SWIM*.

   _____

8. CAN BE SEEN THREE TIMES IN *TATTLE* AND ONCE IN *TOY*.

   _____

9. *HOLY* HAS ONE BUT *HOLLY* HAS TWO.

   _____

10. THIS LETTER IS FOUND IN *GIRLS* BUT NOT *GIRL*.

    _____

"YOU __ILL BE WITH C__I__D AND __IVE BIRTH TO
       7   4 9   2

A S__N, AND __OU A__E __O GIVE HIM THE __AME
    5   6   1   8   3

JE__US.'"
   10

PICTURE CLUES

THE PICTURES ARE YOUR ONLY CLUES TO COMPLETING THIS CROSSWORD. THIS IS A BIT OF A BRAIN TEASER.

UP OR DOWN?

UNSCRAMBLE THE WORDS, THEN IT'S UP TO YOU TO FIND WHERE EACH WORD GOES. WE PUT A FEW LETTERS IN TO HELP.

DBE _____   LTEANBK _____
MLBA _____   YOLHL _____
OEKYND _____ TSRA _____
CWO _____   LBLE _____

11

FIND THE FOUR

COMPLETE THE PUZZLE BELOW BY CROSSING OUT EVERY LETTER THAT APPEARS AT LEAST FOUR TIMES. USE THE REMAINING LETTERS TO COMPLETE THE SENTENCE.

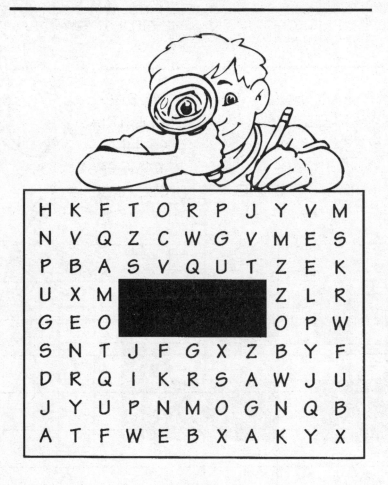

H K F T O R P J Y V M

N V Q Z C W G V M E S

P B A S V Q U T Z E K

U X M ██████████ Z L R

G E O ██████████ O P W

S N T J F G X Z B Y F

D R Q I K R S A W J U

J Y U P N M O G N Q B

A T F W E B X A K Y X

MARY FINDS OUT THAT HER COUSIN, ELIZABETH, WILL ALSO HAVE A __ __ __ __ __ .

TRAVELLIN' RHYMES

THIS IS A GREAT GAME TO PLAY AS YOU TRAVEL. YOU'LL NEED SOMEONE TO PLAY IT WITH, THOUGH, LIKE YOUR BROTHER OR SISTER OR FRIENDS.

BELOW IS A LIST OF WORD PAIRS THAT RHYME WITH EACH OTHER. YOUR JOB IS TO CALL OUT THE WORDS AND HAVE THE PLAYERS COME UP WITH THE SILLIEST RHYMES. WRITE THE BEST ON THE SPACES BELOW.

HAIR, BEAR	TACK, BACK
JUICE, LOOSE	SMILE, TRIAL
RUN, BUN	BIKE, LIKE
ICE, TWICE	ARROW, SPARROW
BALL, HALL	DARK, PARK

_____

_____

_____

_____

_____

_____

_____

_____

PICTURE MAKER

YOU MAKE THE PICTURE. DRAW THE IMAGE FROM EACH FRAME AT THE TOP IN THE FRAME BELOW WITH THE MATCHING NUMBER.

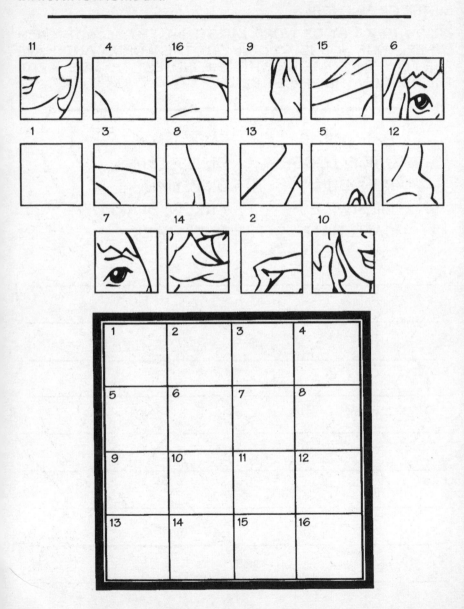

LET'S MAZE AROUND

MARY'S GOING TO VISIT HER COUSIN, ELIZABETH. CAN YOU HELP HER FIND HER WAY?

CAN YOU FIND THE WORDS?

ALL THESE
WORDS ARE HIDDEN IN
THE PUZZLE BELOW.
HAVE FUN!

TREE
KING
MAGI
GALILEE
STAR

INN
JUDEA
CHILD
HEROD
CAMEL

```
            Y  J
            J  K
S  D  W  K  G  F  L  R  K  F  I  W  G  P
   T  C  H  I  L  D  H  N  U  N  D  C
   A  A  S  H  N  B  P  W  S  G  H  A
   X  F  R  D  T  N  B  L  D  J  B  M
   Q  G  D  P  S  V  H  I  O  W  V  E
H  N           L  E  F        N  L
E  W           J  U  S        C  H
R  B           G  U  L  N  B  R  P
O  F        O  Y  T  D  V  I  W  I
D  R           R  T  R  E  E  G  F
T  D           R  T  H  P  A  T  D
Z  F  G  A  L  I  L  E  E  M  A  O  S  M
```

WHERE ARE THOSE VOWELS?

YOU'RE GOING TO HAVE TO CONCENTRATE FOR THIS ONE! VOWELS ARE HIDDEN IN THE PICTURE BELOW. YOU WILL NEED THEM TO COMPLETE THE PUZZLE.

"WH _ N _ L _ Z _ B _ TH H _ _ RD
M _ RY'S GR _ _ _ T _ NG, TH _ B _ BY
L _ _ P _ D _ N H _ R W _ MB, _ ND
_ L _ Z _ B _ TH W _ S F _ LL _ D
W _ TH TH _ H _ LY SP _ R _ T."

LUKE 1:41

17

REALLY SILLY STORIES

YOU CAN PLAY THIS GAME BY YOURSELF, BUT IT'S A LOT MORE FUN TO PLAY WITH OTHERS.

ASK EACH PLAYER TO CALL OUT THE KIND OF WORD INDICATED IN EACH SPACE—A NOUN OR ADJECTIVE OR ADVERB, FOR EXAMPLE—AND PLACE THAT WORD IN THE APPROPRIATE SPACE. DO NOT TELL ANYONE WHAT THE STORY IS ABOUT—IT'S MORE FUN THAT WAY!

BELOW YOU'LL FIND A DESCRIPTION OF WHAT VERBS, NOUNS, ADJECTIVES, ADVERBS, ETC., ARE—JUST IN CASE YOU NEED A LITTLE HELP.

VERB: AN ACTION WORD, LIKE *WALK*, *RUN*, OR *FLY*. MAY BE *WALKED*, *RAN*, OR *FLEW*, IF <u>PAST TENSE</u> IS CALLED FOR.

ADVERB: MODIFIES A VERB AND USUALLY ENDS IN "LY." *SLOWLY* AND *CAREFULLY* ARE A COUPLE OF EXAMPLES.

NOUN: A PERSON, PLACE, OR THING, LIKE *BOY*, *BOAT*, OR *CAR*.

ADJECTIVE: DESCRIBES SOMEONE OR SOMETHING. *DIRTY*, *SILLY*, AND *BIG* ARE A FEW EXAMPLES.

PLACE: COULD BE A *COUNTRY* OR *CITY*, ETC.

PLURAL: MORE THAN ONE ITEM, SUCH AS *GIRLS* IS THE PLURAL OF *GIRL*.

NOW MOVE ON TO THE FOLLOWING PAGE TO PLAY THIS REALLY SILLY GAME!

REALLY SILLY STORIES

DON'T LOOK AT THE STORY BELOW. INSTEAD, FILL IN THE BLANKS IN THE LIST BELOW WITH THE REQUIRED WORDS. THEN FILL IN THE BLANKS IN THE STORY AND GET READY TO LAUGH UNCONTROLLABLY!

PLURAL NOUN _____
ADJECTIVE _____
ADJECTIVE _____
NAME _____
NOUN _____
VERB (PAST TENSE) _____
NOUN _____
ADJECTIVE _____
VERB ENDING IN "ING" _____
VERB (PAST TENSE) _____
ADJECTIVE _____
ADVERB _____

VERB (PAST TENSE) _____
NAME _____
VERB (PAST TENSE) _____
ADJECTIVE _____
VERB _____
NOUN _____
NAME OF SEASON _____
NOUN _____
VERB _____
VERB (PAST TENSE) _____
VERB (PAST TENSE) _____
NOUN _____

THE GRADE SIX _____ AT CENTRAL _____ SCHOOL
          PLURAL NOUN   ADJECTIVE

WERE LOOKING _____ TO THEIR TRIP TO _____
               ADJECTIVE   NAME

MOUNTAIN. THE _____ HAD FINALLY _____ AND
                NOUN   VERB (PAST TENSE)

_____ WAS _____ FOR _____. THEY _____
NOUN   ADJECTIVE   VERB — "ING"   VERB (PAST TENSE)

ON SPENDING THE _____ DAY _____ AND ALL EAGERLY
              ADJECTIVE   ADVERB

_____ THE FUN AHEAD. _____, HOWEVER, WAS
VERB (PAST TENSE)   NAME

_____ ABOUT _____ THING; WOULD HE STILL
VERB (PAST TENSE)   ADJECTIVE

_____ THE _____ TO PERFORM IN THE _____
VERB   NOUN   NAME OF SEASON

PLAY AT HIS _____, LATER IN THE EVENING? HE DIDN'T
         NOUN

_____ TO MISS IT AND _____ HE HADN'T _____ ON
VERB   VERB (PAST TENSE)   VERB (PAST TENSE)

TOO MUCH FOR ONE _____.
             NOUN

19

DON'T LEAVE IT SCRAMBLED!

UNSCRAMBLE EACH WORD, THEN USE THE CIRCLED LETTERS TO COMPLETE THE PUZZLE BELOW . . . AND I HOPE IT DOESN'T HURT YOUR EYES!

"SCBEAEU   SHEOJP   RHE   DSBHNUA

" _ O _ _ _ _ _   _ _ _ _ _ _   _ _ _   _ _ _ _ _ _

SWA A OGRIUHSTE ANM DAN

_ _ _ _ _ _ _ _ _ _ _ O _ _ _ _ _ _ _

IDD TNO TANW OT PSXOEE RHE

_ _ _ O _ _ _ _ _ _ _ O _ _ _ _ _ _ _ _ _

OT UCLPIB AIGERDSC, EH DHA NI

_ _ _ _ O _ _ _ _ _ _ _ _ _ _ _ _ , _ _ _ _ _ _ _

DMNI OT RVOECDI EHR YUQLITE."

_ _ _ _ _ _ _ _ _ _ O _ _ _ _ _ _ _ _ _ _ _ ."

MATTHEW 1:19

WHAT DID JOSEPH PLAN TO DO ABOUT THE WEDDING?

◯ ◯ ◯ ◯ ◯ ◯
_ _ _ _ _ _

20

it's a MYSTERY

THIS IS A GREAT GAME TO PLAY AS YOU TRAVEL. YOU'LL NEED SOMEONE TO PLAY IT WITH, THOUGH, LIKE YOUR BROTHER OR SISTER OR FRIENDS.

BELOW IS A LIST OF PHRASES THAT NEED TO BE COMPLETED. SHOW THIS PUZZLE TO EACH PLAYER, WHO PICKS A LETTER TO FILL IN THE BLANKS, AND THEN HAS TEN SECONDS TO GUESS THE PHRASE. MOVE ON TO EACH PLAYER UNTIL THE MYSTERY IS SOLVED! AS THE HOST OF THIS GAME, YOU GET TO CHECK OUT THE SOLUTION FROM THE ANSWER PAGES AT THE BACK (IF YOU NEED TO)!

T_ _ L_RD _E_ _ S W_ _ _O _ N
_ _ B_ _ _L_H_ _.

_ _E MA_ _ _ B_ _U_ _ _ _ _ _F_S.

T_ _ _E W_S _O _O_ _ _T
_H_ _ _ _N.

A GR_ _ _ _ H_ _T _ _ _ _G_L_
A_ _ _ _A_ _D.

_ _RY, _HE M_ _ _ _ER _F _ _ _E
_ _B_ J_ _ _ _S.

_ _ _ _ _ _D I_ BO_ _ _, _H_
_S _ _R_ _T, _ _ _ LO_ _.

21

C N YOU PICT E IT?

THE PICTURES ARE YOUR CLUES. USE THE CIRCLED LETTERS TO
COMPLETE THE PUZZLE BELOW.

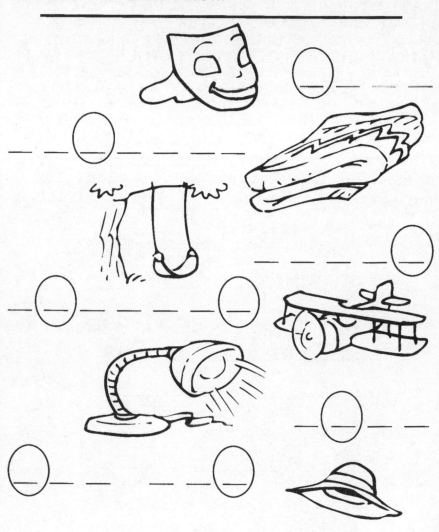

WHO FOLLOWED THE STAR?

◯ ◯ ◯ ◯ FROM THE ◯ ◯ ◯ ◯

UP OR DOWN?

UNSCRAMBLE THE WORDS, THEN IT'S UP TO YOU TO FIND WHERE EACH WORD GOES. WE PUT A FEW LETTERS IN TO HELP.

HSJEPO	_____	ATS	_____
TTNE	_____	NDE	_____
RMREDIA	_____	SJESU	_____
TEBALS	_____	SNO	_____

WHAT CAN I SAY?
I *LOVE* THE WOMAN!

23

WHO, WHAT, WHERE

THIS IS A GREAT GAME TO PLAY AS YOU TRAVEL. YOU'LL NEED SOMEONE TO PLAY IT WITH, THOUGH, LIKE YOUR BROTHER OR SISTER OR FRIENDS.

BELOW IS A LIST OF QUESTIONS THAT NEED A "WHO, WHAT, OR WHERE" ANSWER. EACH PLAYER HAS TEN SECONDS TO ANSWER. AS THE HOST OF THIS GAME, YOU GET TO CHECK OUT THE SOLUTION FROM THE ANSWER PAGES AT THE BACK (IF YOU NEED TO)!

THIS YOUNG GIRL WAS VISITED BY AN ANGEL WITH GOOD NEWS. *WHO* WAS SHE? _____

LUKE 1:26–33

THIS RULER WAS VERY AFRAID OF THE BIRTH OF JESUS CHRIST. *WHO* WAS HE? _____

MATTHEW 2:3

MARY TRAVELLED WITH JOSEPH TO THIS PROVINCE TO GIVE BIRTH. *WHERE* WERE THEY? _____

LUKE 2:4

THIS PLACE WAS FULL, FORCING THE YOUNG COUPLE TO GO ELSEWHERE. *WHAT* WAS IT? _____

LUKE 2:7

HAVING BEEN WARNED, JOSEPH TOOK HIS FAMILY HERE TO LIVE. *WHERE* ARE THEY? _____

MATTHEW 2:13–15

THIS LED MAGI FROM THE EAST TO THE BIRTHPLACE OF CHRIST. *WHAT* WAS IT? _____

MATTHEW 2:9

PICTURE CLUES

THE PICTURES ARE YOUR ONLY CLUES TO COMPLETING THIS
CROSSWORD. THIS IS A BIT OF A BRAIN TEASER.

ALL JUMBLED UP

HEY . . . THIS ONE WILL BE FUN!
FIND THE OPPOSITE OF EACH WORD,
THEN USE THE CIRCLED LETTERS TO
COMPLETE THE PUZZLE BELOW.

MOTHER _ _ _ O _

SUN O _ _ _

PEN _ O _ _ O

DOG _ _O

DAY _ _ _ O _

COLD O _ _

STRAIGHT O _ _ _

TIRED _ _ _ O

WHERE DID THE MIRACLE BEGIN?

O O O O O O O O O

_ _ _ _ _ _ _ _ _

26

PICTURE MAKER

YOU MAKE THE PICTURE. DRAW THE IMAGE FROM EACH
FRAME AT THE TOP IN THE FRAME BELOW WITH THE
MATCHING NUMBER.

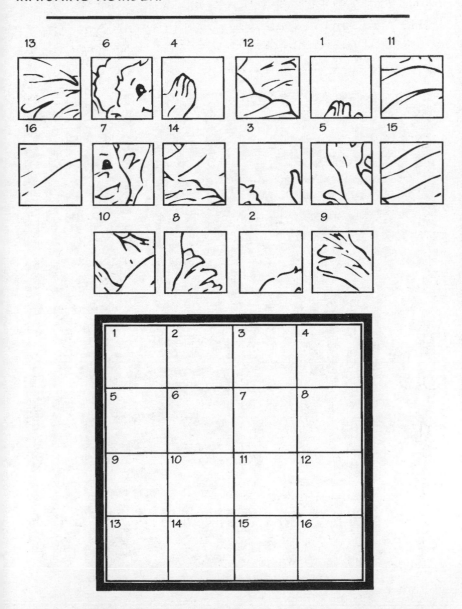

27

LET'S MAZE AROUND

WE ARE IN BETHLEHEM, AND MARY AND JOSEPH NEED HELP FINDING A PLACE FOR HER TO GIVE BIRTH. CAN YOU HELP?

JUST A REGULAR OLD CROSSWORD!

ACROSS

1. HEAVENLY HOST
2. A SPECIAL BABY
3. PLACE FOR ANIMALS
4. CRIB FOR JESUS
5. RIDDEN BY MARY
6. A FALSE GOD

DOWN

1. JOSEPH'S HOMETOWN
2. PROVINCE OF ISRAEL
3. THEY CARE FOR SHEEP
4. LARGE GROUP OF SHEEP
5. THE CREATOR
6. ANCIENT MOTEL

WHERE ARE THOSE VOWELS?

YOU'RE GOING TO HAVE TO CONCENTRATE FOR THIS ONE! VOWELS ARE HIDDEN IN THE PICTURE BELOW. YOU WILL NEED THEM TO COMPLETE THE PUZZLE.

"SH _ _ WR _ PP _ D H _ M _ N
CL _ THS _ ND PL _ C _ D H _ M
_ N _ M _ NG _ R, B _ C _ _ S _
TH _ R _ W _ S N _ R _ _ M
F _ R TH _ M _ N TH _ _ NN."

LUKE 2:7

30

LETTER CLUES

TO DECODE THIS MESSAGE FROM GOD, YOU'LL NEED TO TAKE THE LETTER FROM EACH NUMBERED CLUE AND MATCH IT TO THE NUMBERED SPACE IN THE PUZZLE BELOW.

1. THIS LETTER BEGINS *HAIR* AND ENDS *ROUGH.*
   _____

2. FOUND SECOND TO LAST IN BOTH *LOVE* AND *LEAVE.*
   _____

3. FOUND ONCE IN *CRUMB* AND TWICE IN *ACCEPT.*
   _____

4. THIS ONE'S TWICE IN *EFFECT* BUT ONCE IN *FAIR.*
   _____

5. YOU'LL FIND THIS ONE IN *BEST* BUT NOT IN *BUST.*
   _____

6. YOU'LL FIND THIS TWICE IN *BABY* AND ONCE IN *BOAT.*
   _____

7. THIS LETTER BEGINS *GOAT* AND ENDS *JOG.*
   _____

"AND T__R__ W_R_ S___P___RDS
      1 5 5   5 5   1 5 1 5

LI __ IN __ OUT IN T___ __I__LDS N__AR __Y,
   2   7   1 5   4 5   5   6

K___PIN__ WAT___ O___R T___IR
 5 5   7   3 1   2 5   1 5

__LO__KS AT NI___ __ T."
4   3   7 1

LUKE 2:8

CAN YOU FIND THE WORDS?

ALL THESE WORDS ARE HIDDEN IN THE PUZZLE BELOW. HAVE FUN!

BASKET

CHURCH

TEMPLE

SUNDAY

FLOCK

JOSEPH

BIBLE

STAR

MANGER

MAGI

```
      B W
    S A T
    J S F U
    K Q K Z C V
S T A R N B E S U N D A Y R
G Y E S T R T Z M B K Y C H
  D L M P F P M T W S B N
  V H P J K J A L M I
  U N F L O C K N A B
  B C D Z L E S G Y G L
  P C H U R C H E Q I E
  W Q T J     P Z D R
P H F         H R G
M             K U
```

FIND THE FOUR

COMPLETE THE PUZZLE BELOW BY CROSSING OUT EVERY LETTER THAT APPEARS AT LEAST FOUR TIMES. USE THE REMAINING LETTERS TO COMPLETE THE SENTENCE.

```
M  V  X  K  M  Q  W  R  I  Y
H  G  B  Z  S  C  C  K  E  X
R  P  J  B  F  Z  Q  V  H  R
C  T  Q  W  H  ■  Z  C  D  K
U  K  D  J  U  I  J  S  V  T
W  O  M  Z  O  X  M  D  O  Y
S  N  U  P  Y  L  P  Y  B  F
F  P  X  O  D  R  T  F  Q  V
I  W  T  I  A  J  S  U  H  B
```

AN __ __ __ __ __ APPEARS TO THE SHEPHERDS.

UP OR DOWN?

UNSCRAMBLE THE WORDS, THEN IT'S UP TO YOU TO FIND WHERE EACH WORD GOES. WE PUT A FEW LETTERS IN TO HELP.

ISHHGTE	_____	WCAHT	_____
ONTW	_____	SHTO	_____
GYLRO	_____	DLGA	_____
VLNYEEAH	_____	ISH	_____
DLRO	_____	AEHRT	_____
HNEOS	_____	ERATH	_____

WHO, WHAT, WHERE

THIS IS A GREAT GAME TO PLAY AS YOU TRAVEL. YOU'LL NEED SOMEONE TO PLAY IT WITH, THOUGH, LIKE YOUR BROTHER OR SISTER OR FRIENDS.

BELOW IS A LIST OF QUESTIONS THAT NEED A "WHO, WHAT, OR WHERE" ANSWER. EACH PLAYER HAS TEN SECONDS TO ANSWER. AS THE HOST OF THIS GAME, YOU GET TO CHECK OUT THE SOLUTION FROM THE ANSWER PAGES AT THE BACK (IF YOU NEED TO)!

SHEPHERDS WERE AT WORK, LOOKING AFTER THEIR SHEEP. *WHERE* WERE THEY? _____

LUKE 2:8

SUDDENLY, SOMETHING SHONE ALL AROUND THEM. *WHAT* WAS IT? _____

LUKE 2:9

HE BROUGHT THEM *GOOD NEWS OF GREAT JOY* FOR ALL PEOPLE. *WHO* WAS HE? _____

LUKE 2:10

A SAVIOR HAD BEEN BORN WHO WAS CHRIST, THE LORD. *WHERE* WAS HE BORN? _____

LUKE 2:11

ALL GLORY WAS GIVEN TO HIM BY THE ANGELS AND ALL MEN. *WHO* WAS HE? _____

LUKE 2:14

HE HAD NO BED, BUT THEY FOUND A PLACE TO LAY HIM DOWN. *WHAT* WAS IT? _____

LUKE 2:12

PEACE WAS GIVEN TO THEM ON WHOM RESTED THE FAVOR OF GOD. *WHO* WERE THEY? _____

LUKE 2:14

PICTURE MAKER

YOU MAKE THE PICTURE. DRAW THE IMAGE FROM EACH FRAME AT THE TOP IN THE FRAME BELOW WITH THE MATCHING NUMBER.

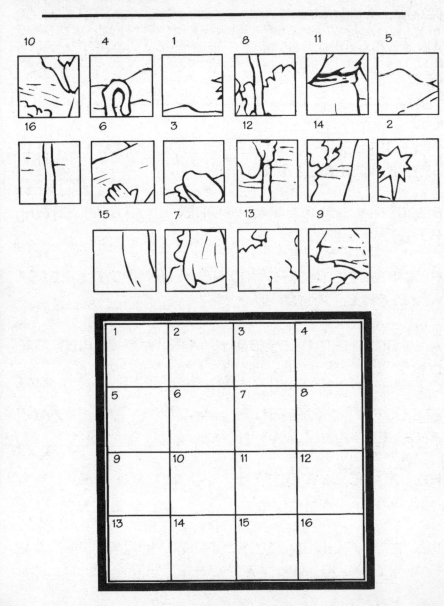

DON'T LEAVE IT SCRAMBLED!

UNSCRAMBLE EACH WORD, THEN USE THE CIRCLED LETTERS TO COMPLETE THE PUZZLE BELOW . . . AND I HOPE IT DOESN'T HURT YOUR EYES!

"LDSUYNDE A RTEAG MCAYNOP FO

_____ _ _(◯)__ _____ __

HET VHNEEAYL STHO EEAARPDP WHTI

___ _(◯)_____ ____ _____ ____

ETH NEALG, IISPRGAN DGO NDA

___ _(◯)____, _____ ___ ___

NASYGI, 'OGLRY OT ODG NI HET

_____, '_____ __ __(◯) __ ___

EIHSTGH, NAD NO TERAH ECPEA

_____(◯)_, ___ __ _____ _(◯)___

OT NME NO OWMH ISH AFRVO

__ ___ __ ____ _(◯)_ _____

TRSES.'"

_____.'"

LUKE 2:13–14

THE HOST OF ANGELS

◯ ◯ ◯ ◯ ◯ ◯ ◯ GOD.

_ _ _ _ _ _ _

REALLY SILLY STORIES

YOU CAN PLAY THIS GAME BY YOURSELF, BUT IT'S A LOT MORE FUN TO PLAY WITH OTHERS.

ASK EACH PLAYER TO CALL OUT THE KIND OF WORD INDICATED IN EACH SPACE—A NOUN OR ADJECTIVE OR ADVERB, FOR EXAMPLE—AND PLACE THAT WORD IN THE APPROPRIATE SPACE. DO NOT TELL ANYONE WHAT THE STORY IS ABOUT— IT'S MORE FUN THAT WAY!

BELOW YOU'LL FIND A DESCRIPTION OF WHAT VERBS, NOUNS, ADJECTIVES, ADVERBS, ETC., ARE—JUST IN CASE YOU NEED A LITTLE HELP.

VERB: AN ACTION WORD, LIKE *WALK, RUN,* OR *FLY.* MAY BE *WALKED, RAN,* OR *FLEW,* IF <u>PAST TENSE</u> IS CALLED FOR.

ADVERB: MODIFIES A VERB AND USUALLY ENDS IN "LY." *SLOWLY* AND *CAREFULLY* ARE A COUPLE OF EXAMPLES.

NOUN: A PERSON, PLACE, OR THING, LIKE *BOY, BOAT,* OR *CAR.*

ADJECTIVE: DESCRIBES SOMEONE OR SOME-THING. *DIRTY, SILLY,* AND *BIG* ARE A FEW EXAMPLES.

PLACE: COULD BE A *COUNTRY* OR *CITY,* ETC.

PLURAL: MORE THAN ONE ITEM, SUCH AS *GIRLS* IS THE PLURAL OF *GIRL.*

NOW MOVE ON TO THE FOLLOWING PAGE TO PLAY THIS REALLY SILLY GAME!

REALLY SILLY STORIES

DON'T LOOK AT THE STORY BELOW. INSTEAD, FILL IN THE BLANKS IN THE LIST BELOW WITH THE REQUIRED WORDS. THEN FILL IN THE BLANKS IN THE STORY AND GET READY TO LAUGH UNCONTROLLABLY!

PLURAL NOUN ——————————
NOUN _____
PLURAL NOUN _____
VERB _____
NOUN _____
NOUN _____
ADJECTIVE _____
PLURAL NOUN _____
VERB ENDING IN "ING" _____
TIME OF DAY _____
PLURAL NOUN _____
PLURAL NOUN _____
PLURAL NOUN _____
VERB (PAST TENSE) _____

VERB _____
ADVERB _____
NOUN _____
PLURAL NOUN _____
NOUN _____
NOUN _____
VERB (PAST TENSE) _____
PLURAL NOUN _____
VERB _____
NOUN _____
NOUN _____
VERB ENDING IN "ING" _____
ADJECTIVE _____

THE _____ FROM THE SUNDAY _____ CLASS WERE
   PLURAL NOUN   NOUN

ALL IN THEIR _____ AND COULD HARDLY _____
         PLURAL NOUN   VERB

THEIR _____. THE _____ WAS ABOUT TO START!
       NOUN   PLURAL NOUN

FOR THE _____ TWO _____, THEY HAD BEEN
         ADJECTIVE   PLURAL NOUN

_____ FOR THIS SPECIAL _____, BUILDING
VERB—"iNG"   TIME OF DAY

_____, SEWING _____, AND LEARNING THEIR
PLURAL NOUN   PLURAL NOUN

_____. THEY WERE _____ IN THEIR RESOLVE
PLURAL NOUN   VERB (PAST TENSE)

TO _____ THIS THE BEST PLAY ANYONE HAD _____
   VERB   ADVERB

SEEN. FINALLY, THE _____ ARRIVED. THE
                       NOUN

_____ DIMMED AND A _____ FELL OVER THE
PLURAL NOUN   NOUN

_____. THE CURTAIN _____ AND THE _____
NOUN   VERB (PAST TENSE)   PLURAL NOUN

WERE GRATIFIED TO _____ THE EXPRESSIONS OF
                VERB

_____ FROM EVERYONE IN THE _____. THIS WAS
NOUN   NOUN

_____ TO BE A _____ NIGHT!
VERB-"ING"   ADJECTIVE

JUST A REGULAR OLD CROSSWORD!

ACROSS
1. JESUS WAS BORN THERE
2. GIVE LIGHT
3. COMPANY OF ANGELS
4. TOWN OF _____
5. THE ANGELS WERE DOING IT

DOWN
1. BORN TO MARY
2. A CARPENTER
3. VERY HIGH
4. VERY AFRAID
5. HE WOULD BRING THIS

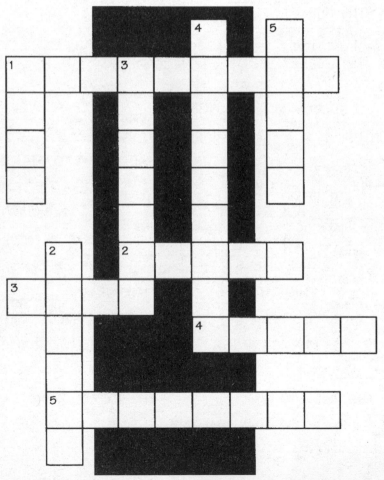

40

TRAVELLIN' RHYMES

THIS IS A GREAT GAME TO PLAY AS YOU TRAVEL. YOU'LL NEED SOMEONE TO PLAY IT WITH, THOUGH, LIKE YOUR BROTHER OR SISTER OR FRIENDS.

BELOW IS A LIST OF WORD PAIRS THAT RHYME WITH EACH OTHER. YOUR JOB IS TO CALL OUT THE WORDS AND HAVE THE PLAYERS COME UP WITH THE SILLIEST RHYMES. WRITE THE BEST ON THE SPACES BELOW.

TRAVEL, GRAVEL	HEART, START
HOST, COAST	CLEANER, MEANER
SUN, FUN	CAR, STAR
CARE, FAIR	BLOW, GROW
BED, SLED	GREETING, MEETING

_____

_____

_____

_____

_____

_____

_____

_____

_____

FIND THE FOUR

COMPLETE THE PUZZLE BELOW BY CROSSING OUT EVERY LETTER THAT APPEARS AT LEAST FOUR TIMES. USE THE REMAINING LETTERS TO COMPLETE THE SENTENCE.

H	E	A	M	B	S	G	P	H	C
C	K	P	J	G	N	F	L	T	J
I	H	R	Q	T	K	U	E	S	N
P	Q	V	K	I	U	B	Y	G	H
F	B	T	W	F	M	Q	V	W	X
J			Y	X	P	S	Y	A	T
M	X	A	E	Q	O	J	I	N	C
V	Y	X	G	U	W	K	C	U	F
A	W	V	I	M	D	B	E	N	S

AT THE TOP . . . *AT THE TOP!*

JESUS IS OUR SAVIOR AND OUR __ __ __ __ .

UP OR DOWN?

UNSCRAMBLE THE WORDS, THEN IT'S UP TO YOU TO FIND WHERE EACH WORD GOES. WE PUT A FEW LETTERS IN TO HELP.

OIRSHPW _____

RADME _____

RHRYM _____

RTMHEO _____

TOYRNCU _____

PPRHOTE _____

FOR YOU!

43

TRAVELLIN' RHYMES

THIS IS A GREAT GAME TO PLAY AS YOU TRAVEL. YOU'LL NEED SOMEONE TO PLAY IT WITH, THOUGH, LIKE YOUR BROTHER OR SISTER OR FRIENDS.

BELOW IS A LIST OF WORD PAIRS THAT RHYME WITH EACH OTHER. YOUR JOB IS TO CALL OUT THE WORDS AND HAVE THE PLAYERS COME UP WITH THE SILLIEST RHYMES. WRITE THE BEST ON THE SPACES BELOW.

MIXTURE, FIXTURE   STRONG, LONG
SALT, MALT   GOOD, HOOD
LAW, SAW   SMILE, WHILE
FEAR, NEAR   STAR, FAR

_____

_____

_____

_____

_____

_____

_____

_____

JUNE... SPOON...
LOON... DUNE...
MOON...

CAN YOU FIND THE WORDS?

ALL THESE
WORDS ARE HIDDEN IN
THE PUZZLE BELOW.
HAVE FUN!

WARNED
DREAM
BOWED
KING
CHILD

MYRRH
TREASURE
GOLD
COUNTRY
REPORT

```
          W D W K
          T A F R
          L H R Z
N B K R F Z V M N E T S K B
G O T R E A S U R E A O I V
C W N E C N O H D F D M N K
J E G O L D R B H R B R G J
  D P L J R M T L O Y T E
  S S Z Y E J P W R G F A
  H M F A V A T E C H
  W D M R N M P B
  P G A U K B O D
  Z V N O E C O R L G
R G K C H I L D T W P S
```

C\`N YOU PICT RE IT?

THE PICTURES ARE YOUR CLUES. USE THE CIRCLED LETTERS TO COMPLETE THE PUZZLE BELOW.

WHAT DID THE ANGEL TELL JOSEPH IN HIS DREAM?

LET'S MAZE AROUND

HEROD WANTS TO FIND THE NEWBORN JESUS AND KILL HIM. HELP THE FAMILY ESCAPE TO EGYPT.

PICTURE MAKER

YOU MAKE THE PICTURE. DRAW THE IMAGE FROM EACH FRAME AT THE TOP IN THE FRAME BELOW WITH THE MATCHING NUMBER.

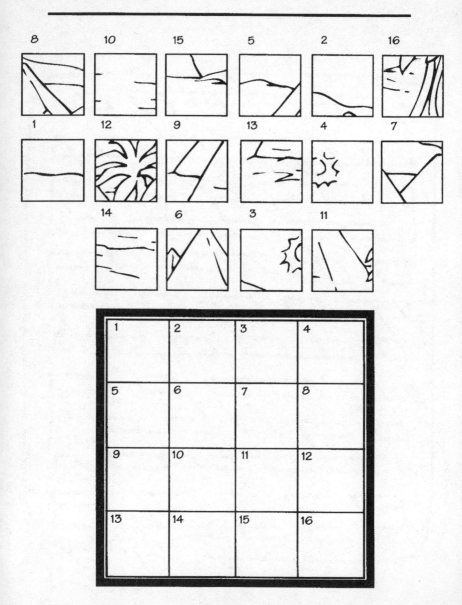

WHO, WHAT, WHERE

THIS IS A GREAT GAME TO PLAY AS YOU TRAVEL. YOU'LL NEED SOMEONE TO PLAY IT WITH, THOUGH, LIKE YOUR BROTHER OR SISTER OR FRIENDS.

BELOW IS A LIST OF QUESTIONS THAT NEED A "WHO, WHAT, OR WHERE" ANSWER. EACH PLAYER HAS TEN SECONDS TO ANSWER. AS THE HOST OF THIS GAME, YOU GET TO CHECK OUT THE SOLUTION FROM THE ANSWER PAGES AT THE BACK (IF YOU NEED TO)!

AN ANGEL TOLD THIS MAN, IN A DREAM, TO ESCAPE TO EGYPT. *WHO* WAS HE? _____

MATTHEW 2:13

THE FAMILY OF JESUS STAYED HERE UNTIL THE DEATH OF HEROD. *WHERE* WERE THEY? _____

MATTHEW 2:14–15

THEY MIGHT HAVE SEEN SOMETHING INCREDIBLE ON ARRIVAL. *WHAT* WAS IT? _____

FIND THE FOUR

COMPLETE THE PUZZLE BELOW BY CROSSING OUT EVERY LETTER THAT APPEARS AT LEAST FOUR TIMES. USE THE REMAINING LETTERS TO COMPLETE THE SENTENCE.

WOW! WHAT A STORY... DON'T YA THINK?

YEAH!

M	B	L	F	T	J	W	M	V	O
I	E	V	C	S	A	P	U	G	Q
K	T	W	N	Q	X	Y	N	X	J
L	G	J	Z	I	Z	L	■	A	Y
C	S	X	B	Z	F	Q	Z	C	B
P	N	R	Y	K	T	N	P	U	G
A	V	M	Q	F	S	G	Y	X	W
U	F	W	L	C	J	B	V	H	M
K	I	D	T	P	U	A	I	K	S

AFTER THE DEATH OF __ __ __ __ __, THE FAMILY OF JESUS RETURNED TO NAZARETH.

PICTURE MAKER

YOU MAKE THE PICTURE. DRAW THE IMAGE FROM EACH FRAME AT THE TOP IN THE FRAME BELOW WITH THE MATCHING NUMBER.

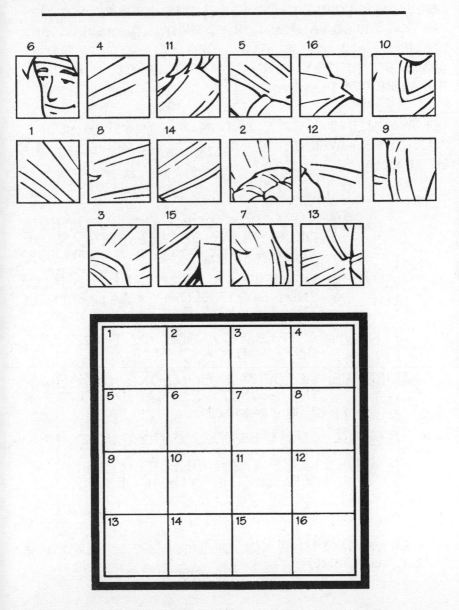

REALLY SILLY STORIES

YOU *CAN* PLAY THIS GAME BY YOURSELF, BUT IT'S A LOT MORE FUN TO PLAY WITH OTHERS.

ASK EACH PLAYER TO CALL OUT THE KIND OF WORD INDICATED IN EACH SPACE—A NOUN OR ADJECTIVE OR ADVERB, FOR EXAMPLE—AND PLACE THAT WORD IN THE APPROPRIATE SPACE. DO NOT TELL ANYONE WHAT THE STORY IS ABOUT—IT'S MORE FUN THAT WAY!

BELOW YOU'LL FIND A DESCRIPTION OF WHAT VERBS, NOUNS, ADJECTIVES, ADVERBS, ETC., ARE—JUST IN CASE YOU NEED A LITTLE HELP.

<u>VERB:</u> AN ACTION WORD, LIKE *WALK, RUN,* OR *FLY.* MAY BE *WALKED, RAN,* OR *FLEW,* IF <u>PAST TENSE</u> IS CALLED FOR.

<u>ADVERB:</u> MODIFIES A VERB AND USUALLY ENDS IN "LY." *SLOWLY* AND *CAREFULLY* ARE A COUPLE OF EXAMPLES.

<u>NOUN:</u> A PERSON, PLACE, OR THING, LIKE *BOY, BOAT,* OR *CAR.*

<u>ADJECTIVE:</u> DESCRIBES SOMEONE OR SOMETHING. *DIRTY, SILLY,* AND *BIG* ARE A FEW EXAMPLES.

<u>PLACE:</u> COULD BE A *COUNTRY* OR *CITY,* ETC.

<u>PLURAL:</u> MORE THAN ONE ITEM, SUCH AS *GIRLS* IS THE PLURAL OF *GIRL.*

NOW MOVE ON TO THE FOLLOWING PAGE TO PLAY THIS REALLY SILLY GAME!

REALLY SILLY STORIES

DON'T LOOK AT THE STORY BELOW. INSTEAD, FILL IN THE BLANKS IN THE LIST BELOW WITH THE REQUIRED WORDS. THEN FILL IN THE BLANKS IN THE STORY AND GET READY TO LAUGH UNCONTROLLABLY!

PLACE _____
ADJECTIVE _____
VERB (PAST TENSE) _____
ADJECTIVE _____
NOUN _____
PLURAL NOUN _____
ADVERB _____
VERB ENDING IN "ING" _____
NOUN _____
PART OF BUILDING _____
PLURAL NOUN_____
ADJECTIVE _____

VERB _____
ADJECTIVE _____
NOUN _____
PLURAL NOUN _____
NOUN _____
ADJECTIVE _____
NOUN _____
PLURAL NOUN _____
VERB (PAST TENSE) _____
PLURAL NOUN _____
NOUN _____
NAME OF SEASON _____

THE CHRISTMAS PLAY AT _____ WAS A _____ HIT!
                          PLACE   ADJECTIVE
WHY, THEY EVEN _____ A _____ _____ AND
                 VERB (PAST TENSE)   ADJECTIVE   NOUN
ALL THE PARENTS AND _____ WERE FULL OF PRAISE
                     PLURAL NOUN
_____. NOW, ALL THE CHILDREN WERE _____
  ADVERB   VERB—"ING"
FORWARD TO THE _____ IN THE MAIN _____. THERE
                  NOUN   PART OF BLDG.
WERE _____ FULL OF ALL KINDS OF _____ THINGS TO
     PLURAL NOUN   ADJECTIVE
_____ AND A WHOLE _____ _____ ENTIRELY FOR
VERB   ADJECTIVE   NOUN
_____. IT WAS STILL EARLY IN THE _____
  PLURAL NOUN   NOUN
AND THE KIDS WERE _____ WITH GREAT ANTICIPATION
                 ADJECTIVE
FOR THE _____ WHEN THEY WERE TO GIVE THE _____
        NOUN   PLURAL NOUN
THEY HAD _____ ON FOR WEEKS, TO THEIR _____.
     VERB (PAST TENSE)   PLURAL NOUN
AFTER ALL, AS THEY HAD LEARNED IN THE _____, GIVING
                                    NOUN
WAS WHAT _____ WAS ALL ABOUT.
     NAME OF SEASON

WHO, WHAT, WHERE

THIS IS A GREAT GAME TO PLAY AS YOU TRAVEL. YOU'LL NEED SOMEONE TO PLAY IT WITH, THOUGH, LIKE YOUR BROTHER OR SISTER OR FRIENDS.

BELOW IS A LIST OF QUESTIONS THAT NEED A "WHO, WHAT, OR WHERE" ANSWER. EACH PLAYER HAS TEN SECONDS TO ANSWER. AS THE HOST OF THIS GAME, YOU GET TO CHECK OUT THE SOLUTION FROM THE ANSWER PAGES AT THE BACK (IF YOU NEED TO)!

THEY TRAVELLED A GREAT DISTANCE TO SEE A NEW-BORN KING. *WHO* WERE THEY? _____

IT IS A MESSAGE OF JOY AND COMES ONCE EVERY YEAR. *WHAT* IS IT? _____

IF THIS KING HAD GOTTEN HIS WAY, THERE WOULD BE NO CHRISTMAS. *WHO* WAS HE? _____

A MIRACULOUS STAR SHONE BRIGHTLY OVER THIS LITTLE TOWN. *WHERE* WAS IT? _____

IT'S ONE WAY WE RE-LIVE THE SPIRIT OF CHRISTMAS WITH LOVED ONES. *WHAT* IS IT? _____

UP OR DOWN?

UNSCRAMBLE THE WORDS, THEN IT'S UP TO YOU TO FIND WHERE EACH WORD GOES. WE PUT A FEW LETTERS IN TO HELP.

GNLEA _____   LKACB _____
MRSISTHAC _____   MIGA _____
_____   EUDAJ _____
YMFALI _____   TGSFI _____
VROSAI _____   LDGA _____
NMGIDKO _____

55

REALLY SILLY STORIES

YOU *CAN* PLAY THIS GAME BY YOURSELF, BUT IT'S A LOT MORE FUN TO PLAY WITH OTHERS.

ASK EACH PLAYER TO CALL OUT THE KIND OF WORD INDICATED IN EACH SPACE—A NOUN OR ADJECTIVE OR ADVERB, FOR EXAMPLE—AND PLACE THAT WORD IN THE APPROPRIATE SPACE. DO NOT TELL ANYONE WHAT THE STORY IS ABOUT—IT'S MORE FUN THAT WAY!

BELOW YOU'LL FIND A DESCRIPTION OF WHAT VERBS, NOUNS, ADJECTIVES, ADVERBS, ETC., ARE—JUST IN CASE YOU NEED A LITTLE HELP.

<u>VERB:</u> AN ACTION WORD, LIKE *WALK, RUN,* OR *FLY.* MAY BE *WALKED, RAN,* OR *FLEW,* IF <u>PAST TENSE</u> IS CALLED FOR.

<u>ADVERB:</u> MODIFIES A VERB AND USUALLY ENDS IN "LY." *SLOWLY* AND *CAREFULLY* ARE A COUPLE OF EXAMPLES.

<u>NOUN:</u> A PERSON, PLACE, OR THING, LIKE *BOY, BOAT,* OR *CAR.*

<u>ADJECTIVE:</u> DESCRIBES SOMEONE OR SOMETHING. *DIRTY, SILLY,* AND *BIG* ARE A FEW EXAMPLES.

<u>PLACE:</u> COULD BE A *COUNTRY* OR *CITY,* ETC.

<u>PLURAL:</u> MORE THAN ONE ITEM, SUCH AS *GIRLS* IS THE PLURAL OF *GIRL.*

NOW MOVE ON TO THE FOLLOWING PAGE TO PLAY THIS REALLY SILLY GAME!

REALLY SILLY STORIES

DON'T LOOK AT THE STORY BELOW. INSTEAD, FILL IN THE BLANKS IN THE LIST BELOW WITH THE REQUIRED WORDS. THEN FILL IN THE BLANKS IN THE STORY AND GET READY TO LAUGH UNCONTROLLABLY!

VERB (PAST TENSE) _____

VERB _____

NUMBER _____

NAME OF SEASON _____

VERB (PAST TENSE) _____

NOUN _____

NOUN _____

VERB ENDING IN "ING" _____

VERB (PAST TENSE) _____

PLURAL NOUN _____

VERB (PAST TENSE) _____

PLURAL NOUN _____

NOUN _____

VERB ENDING IN "ING" _____

NOUN _____

VERB (PAST TENSE) _____

NOUN _____

VERB _____

THE DAY THAT MICHELLE _____ HAD FINALLY COME.
　　　　　　　　　　　　　VERB (PAST TENSE)

SHE COULD NOT _____ OFF ANY LONGER, ESPECIALLY
　　　　　　　　　　VERB

WHEN THERE WERE ONLY _____ DAYS LEFT UNTIL
　　　　　　　　　　　　　NUMBER

_____ EVE. SHE HAD JUST _____ HER
NAME OF SEASON　　　　　　　　　　　VERB (PAST TENSE)

_____ AND SO, IT WAS OFF TO THE _____ TO
NOUN　　　　　　　　　　　　　　　　　　　NOUN

DO HER CHRISTMAS _____. AS SHE _____
　　　　　　　　　VERB—"ING"　　　　　　VERB (PAST TENSE)

THROUGH THE MAIN ENTRANCE _____, SHE WAS
　　　　　　　　　　　　　　PLURAL NOUN

_____ BY THE _____ AND THE _____, BUT,
VERB (PAST TENSE)　　PLURAL NOUN　　　　　NOUN

_____ HER _____ AND RESOLVE, SHE
VERB—"ING"　　　　　　NOUN

_____ INTO THE CRUSHING _____. SHE
VERB (PAST TENSE)　　　　　　　　　　　NOUN

PRAYED SHE WOULD _____ THE DAY.
　　　　　　　　　VERB

57

LET'S MAZE AROUND

CHRISTMAS IN A SHOPPING MALL—WHAT A CRAZY PLACE TO BE! HELP THE FAMILY FIND THEIR WAY THROUGH.

TRAVELLIN' RHYMES

THIS IS A GREAT GAME TO PLAY AS YOU TRAVEL. YOU'LL NEED SOMEONE TO PLAY IT WITH, THOUGH, LIKE YOUR BROTHER OR SISTER OR FRIENDS.

BELOW IS A LIST OF WORD PAIRS THAT RHYME WITH EACH OTHER. YOUR JOB IS TO CALL OUT THE WORDS AND HAVE THE PLAYERS COME UP WITH THE SILLIEST RHYMES. WRITE THE BEST ON THE SPACES BELOW.

PRESENT, PHEASANT   LIGHT, MIGHT
DOOR, SNORE   GLASS, GRASS
PLUM, YUM   GLOW, SNOW
FRIEND, LEND   TREE, BEE

_____

_____

_____

_____

_____

_____

_____

CAN YOU PICTURE IT?

THE PICTURES ARE YOUR CLUES. USE THE CIRCLED LETTERS TO
COMPLETE THE PUZZLE BELOW.

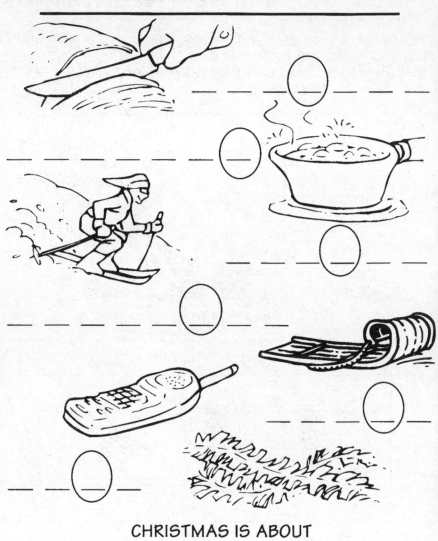

CHRISTMAS IS ABOUT

◯ ◯ ◯ ◯ ◯ ◯,
‾ ‾ ‾ ‾ ‾ ‾

NOT GETTING.

PICTURE CLUES

THE PICTURES ARE YOUR ONLY CLUES TO COMPLETING THIS CROSSWORD. THIS IS A BIT OF A BRAIN TEASER.

FIND THE FOUR

COMPLETE THE PUZZLE BELOW BY CROSSING OUT EVERY LETTER THAT APPEARS AT LEAST FOUR TIMES. USE THE REMAINING LETTERS TO COMPLETE THE SENTENCE.

WHERE'S JESUS?

A	N	B	P	E	R	D	M	J	N
K	Q	U	S	C	Q	X	V	A	L
M	J	H	W	Y		G	S	H	O
C	O	V	K		K	W	U	Y	B
R	X	P	Y	F	X	N	E	K	D
P	S	Y	C	L	Q	M	A	X	Q
D	V	I	E	B	J	S	R	H	W
O	H	N	R	W	V	O	B	L	T
J	L	A	U	D	P	C	U	M	E

JESUS IS OUR __ __ __ __ FROM GOD.

CAN YOU FIND THE WORDS?

ALL THESE WORDS ARE HIDDEN IN THE PUZZLE BELOW. HAVE FUN!

CHRISTMAS   SPECIAL
BETHLEHEM   MALL
ANGELS   SHOPPING
STAR   SPENDING
HOLIDAY   GLORY
CONCERT   JESUS

```
        H M W B
      A   N Q K R G
    C O N C E R T P Y
  H L S D G F V S R D H C
  O N J P T E L O T L S M
  L F R E H M L K S A T A J
B I S V F S G Q S M F R L S
K D G R Z L U J T Z V M L P
G A Q W C W S S F K C A R E
J Y P N F Q I Z D K I N L N
D M S T V R J V W C R G T D
  B E T H L E H E M H S P I
    F C M P L P J Q B D C N
      K B H S H O P P I N G
```

JUST A REGULAR OLD CROSSWORD!

ACROSS

1. WHERE LOVE DWELLS
2. ACT OF GOD
3. TO ADORN
4. FOR WALKING ON SNOW
5. TO SHINE BRIGHTLY

DOWN

1. LIKE A BROTHER
2. CARING ACT
3. BIND TOGETHER
4. JESUS GIVES IT TO US
5. TO JOIN CLOTH

64

PICTURE MAKER

YOU MAKE THE PICTURE. DRAW THE IMAGE FROM EACH FRAME AT THE TOP IN THE FRAME BELOW WITH THE MATCHING NUMBER.

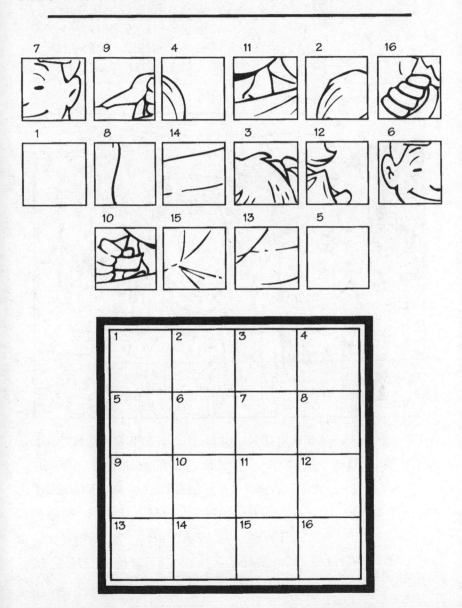

WHERE ARE THOSE VOWELS?

YOU'RE GOING TO HAVE TO CONCENTRATE FOR THIS ONE! VOWELS ARE HIDDEN IN THE PICTURE BELOW. YOU WILL NEED THEM TO COMPLETE THE PUZZLE.

"AFTER JESUS WAS B __ RN __ N BETHLEHEM __ N JUDEA, DUR __ NG THE T __ ME __ F K __ NG HER __ D, MAG __ FR __ M THE EAST CAME T __ JERUSALEM AND ASKED, 'WHERE __ S THE __ NE WH __ HAS BEEN B __ RN K __ NG __ F THE JEWS? WE SAW H __ S STAR __ N THE EAST AND HAVE C __ ME T __ W __ RSH __ P H __ M.'"

MATTHEW 2:1–2

66

LESS SHALL BE FIRST

PLACE THE WORDS BELOW INTO THE PUZZLE ACCORDING TO THE NUMBER OF LETTERS IN EACH WORD, BEGINNING WITH THE WORD THAT HAS THE FEWEST LETTERS. THEN, UNSCRAMBLE THE CIRCLED LETTERS TO COMPLETE THE ANSWER BELOW.

FRIENDS   HOT
GLORY   MOTHER
TRIMMINGS   PRESENTS
BAND   TELEVISION

TO ◯ ◯ ◯ ◯ IS

◯ ◯ ◯ ◯ ◯ THAN TO RECEIVE!

REALLY SILLY STORIES

YOU CAN PLAY THIS GAME BY YOURSELF, BUT IT'S A LOT MORE FUN TO PLAY WITH OTHERS.

ASK EACH PLAYER TO CALL OUT THE KIND OF WORD INDICATED IN EACH SPACE—A NOUN OR ADJECTIVE OR ADVERB, FOR EXAMPLE—AND PLACE THAT WORD IN THE APPROPRIATE SPACE. DO NOT TELL ANYONE WHAT THE STORY IS ABOUT—IT'S MORE FUN THAT WAY!

BELOW YOU'LL FIND A DESCRIPTION OF WHAT VERBS, NOUNS, ADJECTIVES, ADVERBS, ETC., ARE—JUST IN CASE YOU NEED A LITTLE HELP.

<u>VERB:</u> AN ACTION WORD, LIKE *WALK, RUN,* OR *FLY.* MAY BE *WALKED, RAN,* OR *FLEW,* IF <u>PAST TENSE</u> IS CALLED FOR.

<u>ADVERB:</u> MODIFIES A VERB AND USUALLY ENDS IN "LY." *SLOWLY* AND *CAREFULLY* ARE A COUPLE OF EXAMPLES.

<u>NOUN:</u> A PERSON, PLACE, OR THING, LIKE *BOY, BOAT,* OR *CAR.*

<u>ADJECTIVE:</u> DESCRIBES SOMEONE OR SOMETHING. *DIRTY, SILLY,* AND *BIG* ARE A FEW EXAMPLES.

<u>PLACE:</u> COULD BE A *COUNTRY* OR *CITY,* ETC.

<u>PLURAL:</u> MORE THAN ONE ITEM, SUCH AS *GIRLS* IS THE PLURAL OF *GIRL.*

NOW MOVE ON TO THE FOLLOWING PAGE TO PLAY THIS REALLY SILLY GAME!

REALLY SILLY STORIES

DON'T LOOK AT THE STORY BELOW. INSTEAD, FILL IN THE BLANKS IN THE LIST BELOW WITH THE REQUIRED WORDS. THEN FILL IN THE BLANKS IN THE STORY AND GET READY TO LAUGH UNCONTROLLABLY!

PLURAL NOUN _____
VERB (PAST TENSE)
_____
NOUN _____
ADJECTIVE
NOUN _____
ADJECTIVE _____
NOUN _____
VERB (PAST TENSE)
_____
PLURAL NOUN _____
ADVERB _____
NOUN _____

VERB _____
NOUN _____
ADJECTIVE _____
PLURAL NOUN _____
ADJECTIVE _____
NOUN _____
NOUN _____
NOUN _____
NOUN _____
NOUN _____
TIME OF DAY _____
PLURAL NOUN _____
NOUN _____

THE _____ HAD _____ A WONDERFUL TIME AT
   PLURAL NOUN   VERB (PAST TENSE)

_____ THIS CHRISTMAS EVE, BUT WERE _____ TO BE
NOUN   ADJECTIVE

FINALLY _____ AFTER A _____ AND BUSY _____.
      NOUN   ADJECTIVE   NOUN

EVERYONE _____ IN, CHANGING INTO THEIR
          VERB (PAST TENSE)

_____, LOOKING _____ TO THE
   PLURAL NOUN   ADVERB

HOT _____ THEY WOULD _____ BEFORE THE _____.
    NOUN   VERB   NOUN

MOM AND DAD WERE ESPECIALLY _____, AS THEIR
                        ADJECTIVE

_____ WERE STILL _____ AND THEY FOUND
  PLURAL NOUN   ADJECTIVE

MUCH _____ IN THEIR KIDS' _____ AND
     NOUN   NOUN

_____ ABOUT THE SEASON. THEY WOULD READ
   NOUN

FROM THE _____, THE TRUE _____ OF THIS _____
       NOUN   NOUN   TIME OF DAY

SO THAT THE _____ WOULD KNOW WHAT ALL

_____ WAS REALLY ABOUT.
   NOUN

LETTER CLUES

TO DECODE THIS MESSAGE FROM GOD, YOU'LL NEED TO TAKE THE LETTER FROM EACH NUMBERED CLUE AND MATCH IT TO THE NUMBERED SPACE IN THE PUZZLE BELOW.

1. THIS LETTER IS FOUND BOTH IN *BIN* AND IN *TRIM*.
   _____

2. THIS LETTER BEGINS BOTH THE WORDS *DESK* AND *DOG*.
   _____

3. THIS LETTER IS FOUND IN *TALK* BUT NOT IN *WALK*.
   _____

4. THIS LETTER IS FOUND IN *MAZE* BUT NOT IN *HAZE*.
   _____

5. IT APPEARS TWICE IN *BABY* AND ONCE IN *BELL*.
   _____

6. THIS LETTER IS FOUND IN *WING* BUT NOT IN *SING*.
   _____

7. THE SAME LETTER IS FOUND ONCE IN *COARSE* AND IN *SIT*.
   _____

"_ H _ _   _ _   H O _   _ H E   _ _ R _ H   O F
  3 1 7   1 7   6   3   5 1 3

J E _ U _   C H R _ _ _ _   C A _ E   A _ O U _ :   H _ _
    7 7   1 7 3   4   5   3   1 7

_ O _ H E R   _ A R Y   _ A _   P L E _ G E _   _ O
4 3   4   6 7   2   2   3

_ E _ A R R _ E _   _ O   J O _ E P H,   _ U _
5   4   1 2   3   7   5 3

_ E F O R E   _ H E Y   C A _ E   _ O G E _ H E R,
5   3   4   3   3

_ H E   _ A _   F O U N _   _ O   _ E   _ _ _ H
7   6 7   2   3   5   6 1 3

C H _ L _   _ H R O U G H   _ H E   H O L Y
   1 2   3   3

_ P _ R _ _ ."
7 1   1 3

WHO, WHAT, WHERE

THIS IS A GREAT GAME TO PLAY AS YOU TRAVEL. YOU'LL NEED SOMEONE TO PLAY IT WITH, THOUGH, LIKE YOUR BROTHER OR SISTER OR FRIENDS.

BELOW IS A LIST OF QUESTIONS THAT NEED A "WHO, WHAT, OR WHERE" ANSWER. EACH PLAYER HAS TEN SECONDS TO ANSWER. AS THE HOST OF THIS GAME, YOU GET TO CHECK OUT THE SOLUTION FROM THE ANSWER PAGES AT THE BACK (IF YOU NEED TO)!

HE ASKED THE MAGI TO RETURN TO HIM, AS HE HAD EVIL IN MIND. *WHO* WAS HE? _____

HE GREW FROM HUMBLE BEGINNINGS TO BE THE SAVIOR OF ALL. *WHO* WAS HE? _____

JESUS' FAMILY RETURNED TO LIVE HERE AFTER EXILE IN EGYPT. *WHERE* WERE THEY?

_____

IT LED THESE MEN OVER A LONG DISTANCE TO SEE A MIRACLE. *WHAT* WAS IT? _____

THROUGH HIS POWER, MARY CONCEIVED A BLESSED CHILD. *WHO* WAS HE? _____

THE MAGI BROUGHT SOMETHING SPECIAL TO JESUS. *WHAT* WAS IT? _____

WHERE ARE THOSE VOWELS?

YOU'RE GOING TO HAVE TO CONCENTRATE FOR THIS ONE! VOWELS ARE HIDDEN IN THE PICTURE BELOW. YOU WILL NEED THEM TO COMPLETE THE PUZZLE.

TH__ B__ST PR__S__NT W__ H__V__ __V__R R__C____V__D __S J__S__S. H__ __S G__D'S GR____T__ST G__FT T__ __S, G__V__N __N L__V__ T__ __LL P____PL__.

it's a MYSTERY

THIS IS A GREAT GAME TO PLAY AS YOU TRAVEL. YOU'LL NEED SOMEONE TO PLAY IT WITH, THOUGH, LIKE YOUR BROTHER OR SISTER OR FRIENDS.

BELOW IS A LIST OF PHRASES THAT NEED TO BE COMPLETED. SHOW THIS PUZZLE TO EACH PLAYER, WHO PICKS A LETTER TO FILL IN THE BLANKS, AND THEN HAS TEN SECONDS TO GUESS THE PHRASE. MOVE ON TO EACH PLAYER UNTIL THE MYSTERY IS SOLVED! AS THE HOST OF THIS GAME, YOU GET TO CHECK OUT THE SOLUTION FROM THE ANSWER PAGES AT THE BACK (IF YOU NEED TO)!

_ _ E   B _ _ T   _ _ _ S E _ _
_ _ _ R.

_ _ _   _ I _ _   _ F _ H _ _ E W _.

_ A _ A R _ _ _,   A T _ _ _   _ _
_ _ L _ _ _ E.

_ _ O R _   T _   _ _ D   _ _   T _ _
H _ _ _ E _ T.

_ H _   _ N _ E _   _ _   _ _ _
_ O _ _.

73

PICTURE MAKER

YOU MAKE THE PICTURE. DRAW THE IMAGE FROM EACH FRAME AT THE TOP IN THE FRAME BELOW WITH THE MATCHING NUMBER.

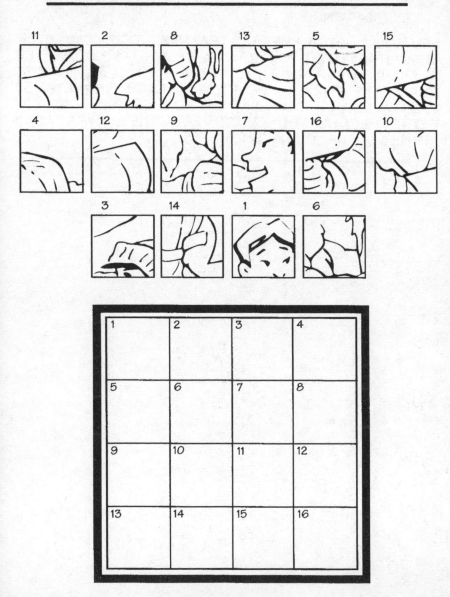

ALL JUMBLED UP

HEY . . . THIS ONE WILL BE FUN!
FIND THE OPPOSITE OF EACH WORD,
THEN USE THE CIRCLED LETTERS TO
COMPLETE THE PUZZLE BELOW.

GO   _ (_) _ _

BROTHER   _ (_) _ (_) _ _

AUNT   _ (_) _ _

WRAP   _ _ _ _ (_) _

BLACK   _ _ (_) _ _

FULL   _ _ _ _ _ (_)

STAY   _ _ (_) _

A WELL KNOWN CHRISTMAS EVENT.

(_) (_) (_) (_) (_) (_) (_) (_)

75

UP OR DOWN?

UNSCRAMBLE THE WORDS, THEN IT'S UP TO YOU TO FIND WHERE EACH WORD GOES. WE PUT A FEW LETTERS IN TO HELP.

CWHTA _____

EHLBTEMHE

_____

OYHL _____

TRSA _____

VREALT _____

NLPA _____

TRAAZHEN _____

EMRAD _____

NRWSEA _____

HEOP _____

FIND THE FOUR

COMPLETE THE PUZZLE BELOW BY CROSSING OUT EVERY LETTER THAT APPEARS AT LEAST FOUR TIMES. USE THE REMAINING LETTERS TO COMPLETE THE SENTENCE.

D	I	P	F	M	Q	O	C	H	W
S	G	J	U	X	N	V	W	K	F
L	W	O	B	Y	Z	D	E	S	L
N	H	K	■	C	U	Z	Q	N	Y
C	Q	S	Z	A	I	K	L	V	C
B	M	Y	P	K	Y	B	M	X	V
U	I	T	J	H	U	D	P	O	I
F	O	V	Q	X	L	X	Z	J	D
J	W	B	N	F	M	R	S	H	P

IF EVERYONE PITCHES IN, ALL WILL HAVE A
_ _ _ _ _ DAY!

LET'S MAZE AROUND

THE FAMILY IS HEADING TO GRANDMA'S FOR CHRISTMAS DINNER. HELP THEM GET THROUGH THE BUSY STREETS.

TRAVELLIN' RHYMES

THIS IS A GREAT GAME TO PLAY AS YOU TRAVEL. YOU'LL NEED SOMEONE TO PLAY IT WITH, THOUGH, LIKE YOUR BROTHER OR SISTER OR FRIENDS.

BELOW IS A LIST OF WORD PAIRS THAT RHYME WITH EACH OTHER. YOUR JOB IS TO CALL OUT THE WORDS AND HAVE THE PLAYERS COME UP WITH THE SILLIEST RHYMES. WRITE THE BEST ON THE SPACES BELOW.

STAIR, HAIR
GOOSE, JUICE
TRUCK, LUCK
PUCK, DUCK
RUG, PLUG

CONE, PHONE
SPEAK, BEAK
STAND, BAND
CHAIR, GLARE
GIVING, LIVING

_____

_____

_____

_____

_____

_____

_____

_____

LESS SHALL BE FIRST

PLACE THE WORDS BELOW INTO THE PUZZLE ACCORDING TO THE NUMBER OF LETTERS IN EACH WORD, BEGINNING WITH THE WORD THAT HAS THE FEWEST LETTERS. THEN, UNSCRAMBLE THE CIRCLED LETTERS TO COMPLETE THE ANSWER BELOW.

MIRACLE   SKIING
BREAD   CHOCOLATE
NATIVITY   HOLY
GAB

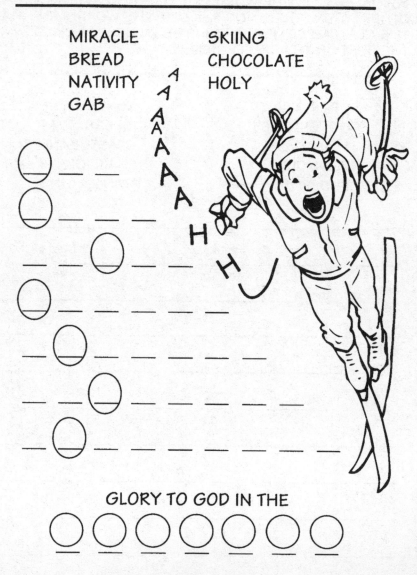

GLORY TO GOD IN THE

CAN YOU FIND THE WORDS?

ALL THESE
WORDS ARE HIDDEN IN
THE PUZZLE BELOW.
HAVE FUN!

CHILDREN
MOTHER
FATHER
BROTHER
SISTER

AUNT
UNCLE
GRANDMA
GRANDPA
FRIENDS

```
      C K G
      H N P V D Q R F G
  V G R A N D M A T C J
  S H M B R L O R U V W M G P
  F I S W Q X T H Z N B X R P
  L T S F A T H E R Y T S A K
  G P L T J C E D K W D F N S
  N V K C E G R L Y N B E D R
  B U Z X N R H M E D R B P C
  Q N Y V J Q I R D O Z A G
      T C Z P R W L N T H J M
      R X L F S I C T H L W T
      D M E H Y B K E Y F B
      J G C Q F D X R S N P
```

JUST A REGULAR OLD CROSSWORD!

ACROSS

1. PURPOSE OF MALL
2. SEED OF A TREE
3. STRINGED INSTRUMENT
4. WINTER VEHICLE
5. JOYOUS EXPRESSION
6. DONE WITH A BOOK

DOWN

1. VOCAL MELODY
2. COLDEST SEASON
3. QUIET MANNER
4. GIVEN TO GOD
5. BETTER THAN POTS
6. CREATOR

LET'S MAZE AROUND

HELP THE MAGI FIND THE BEST ROUTE TO BETHLEHEM.

ALL JUMBLED UP

HEY . . . THIS ONE WILL BE FUN!
FIND THE OPPOSITE OF EACH WORD,
THEN USE THE CIRCLED LETTERS TO
COMPLETE THE PUZZLE BELOW.

FATHER   ◯ _ _ _ _ _

SHORT   _ ◯ _ _ _

SICK   _ ◯ _ _

WEEDS   ◯ _ _ _ _

GRANDMA   _ _ _ _ ◯ _ _ _

ADD   _ _ _ ◯ _ _ _

WHERE WAS THE BABY JESUS BORN?

◯ ◯ ◯ ◯ ◯ ◯
_ _ _ _ _ _

84

PICTURE MAKER

YOU MAKE THE PICTURE. DRAW THE IMAGE FROM EACH FRAME AT THE TOP IN THE FRAME BELOW WITH THE MATCHING NUMBER.

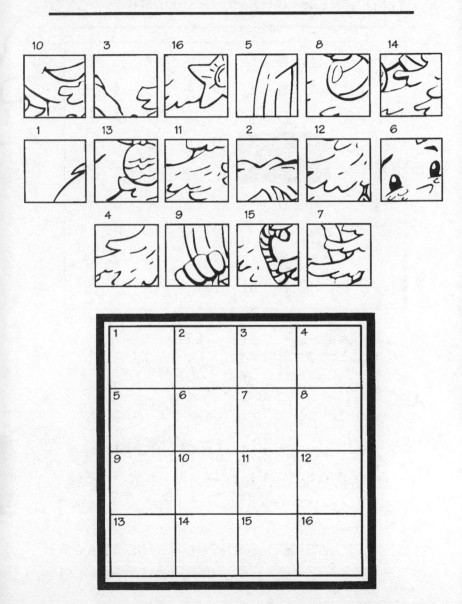

COMPLETE THE PUZZLE BELOW BY CROSSING OUT EVERY LETTER THAT APPEARS AT LEAST FOUR TIMES. USE THE REMAINING LETTERS TO COMPLETE THE SENTENCE.

F	Q	J	K	N	U	A	M	F	P
P	E	V	S	L	G	V	L	U	H
I	S	N	B	F	Y	Z	W	D	U
M	G				W	H	N	X	K
K	X			O	Z	Y	S	G	
H	Z	R	J	I	Q	Y	X	I	B
L	B	W	Z	Y	P	W	F	T	M
V	N	X	S	H	U	C	V	Q	J
Q	I	P	B	M	J	K	G	L	E

THE KIDS WERE OLD ENOUGH THIS YEAR TO

_ _ _ _ _ _ _ _ THE TREE THEMSELVES.

PICTURE CLUES

THE PICTURES ARE YOUR ONLY CLUES TO COMPLETING THIS CROSSWORD. THIS IS A BIT OF A BRAIN TEASER.

AN YOU PICT RE IT?

THE PICTURES ARE YOUR CLUES. USE THE CIRCLED LETTERS TO COMPLETE THE PUZZLE BELOW.

LOOK ◯ ◯ ◯ ◯ ◯ ◯ ◯
_ _ _ _ _ _ _
TO SEE WHAT JOY YOUR PRESENTS BRING.

DON'T LEAVE IT SCRAMBLED!

UNSCRAMBLE EACH WORD, THEN USE THE CIRCLED LETTERS TO COMPLETE THE PUZZLE BELOW . . . AND I HOPE IT DOESN'T HURT YOUR EYES!

"RLYOG OT DGO NI HET SGEHITH, NAD

" _____ __ ___ __ __ ◯_____, ___

NO ATREH CEEPA OT ENM NO OWMH

__ _____ __◯_◯_ ___ __ ____

ISH VOAFR TRSES."

_◯_ _____ ◯___◯."

AWESOME!!

LUKE 2:14

THE GREATEST GIFT?

◯◯◯◯◯◯
_____

89

PICTURE MAKER

YOU MAKE THE PICTURE. DRAW THE IMAGE FROM EACH FRAME AT THE TOP IN THE FRAME BELOW WITH THE MATCHING NUMBER.

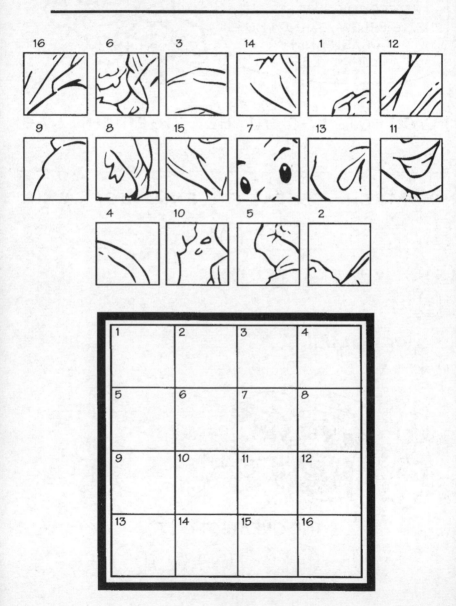

DON'T LEAVE IT SCRAMBLED!

UNSCRAMBLE EACH WORD, THEN USE THE CIRCLED LETTERS TO COMPLETE THE PUZZLE BELOW ... AND I HOPE IT DOESN'T HURT YOUR EYES!

SA   OGD   EGVA   OYU   IHS   ETSB

NERESPT,   UYO   OTO   LOUHDS   IGEV

OT   HRTEOS   ROYU   OELV   DAN

NNDISESK.   OT   IVEG   TISH   OT

HNTOERA   SI   RAF   OREM   BAAULLVE

TANH   YGNHITNA   LESE.

GIVE YOUR BEST

◯ ◯ ◯ ◯ ◯ ◯.

91

REALLY SILLY STORIES

YOU CAN PLAY THIS GAME BY YOURSELF, BUT IT'S A LOT MORE FUN TO PLAY WITH OTHERS.

ASK EACH PLAYER TO CALL OUT THE KIND OF WORD INDICATED IN EACH SPACE—A NOUN OR ADJECTIVE OR ADVERB, FOR EXAMPLE—AND PLACE THAT WORD IN THE APPROPRIATE SPACE. DO NOT TELL ANYONE WHAT THE STORY IS ABOUT—IT'S MORE FUN THAT WAY!

BELOW YOU'LL FIND A DESCRIPTION OF WHAT VERBS, NOUNS, ADJECTIVES, ADVERBS, ETC., ARE—JUST IN CASE YOU NEED A LITTLE HELP.

VERB: AN ACTION WORD, LIKE *WALK*, *RUN*, OR *FLY*. MAY BE *WALKED*, *RAN*, OR *FLEW*, IF <u>PAST TENSE</u> IS CALLED FOR.

ADVERB: MODIFIES A VERB AND USUALLY ENDS IN "LY." *SLOWLY* AND *CAREFULLY* ARE A COUPLE OF EXAMPLES.

NOUN: A PERSON, PLACE, OR THING, LIKE *BOY*, *BOAT*, OR *CAR*.

ADJECTIVE: DESCRIBES SOMEONE OR SOMETHING. *DIRTY*, *SILLY*, AND *BIG* ARE A FEW EXAMPLES.

PLACE: COULD BE A *COUNTRY* OR *CITY*, ETC.

PLURAL: MORE THAN ONE ITEM, SUCH AS *GIRLS* IS THE PLURAL OF *GIRL*.

NOW MOVE ON TO THE FOLLOWING PAGE TO PLAY THIS REALLY SILLY GAME!

REALLY SILLY STORIES

DON'T LOOK AT THE STORY BELOW. INSTEAD, FILL IN THE BLANKS IN THE LIST BELOW WITH THE REQUIRED WORDS. THEN FILL IN THE BLANKS IN THE STORY AND GET READY TO LAUGH UNCONTROLLABLY!

TIME OF DAY _____

NOUN _____

NOUN _____

PLURAL NOUN _____

NOUN _____

NOUN _____

NOUN _____

PLURAL NOUN _____

PLURAL NOUN _____

ADJECTIVE _____

VERB ENDING IN "ING" _____

PLURAL NOUN _____

PLURAL NOUN _____

NOUN _____

VERB _____

PLURAL NOUN _____

VERB _____

VERB ENDING IN "ING" _____

NAME OF SEASON _____

PLURAL NOUN _____

VERB ENDING IN "ING" _____

VERB ENDING IN "ING" _____

CHRISTMAS _____ HAD FINALLY ARRIVED AND THE
         TIME OF DAY

_____ WAS IN THE _____ OF UNWRAPPING THE
   NOUN   NOUN

_____ UNDER THE _____. THERE WAS A
   PLURAL NOUN   NOUN

LOT OF _____ BEING TOGETHER AND MUCH _____
          NOUN   NOUN

AS THEY EXCHANGED _____. THE _____ WERE
                        PLURAL NOUN   PLURAL NOUN

PLEASED AS THEY NOTICED THEIR KIDS SEEMING TO BE

MORE _____ ABOUT THE _____ OF THE _____
        ADJECTIVE   VERB—"ING"   PLURAL NOUN

RATHER THAN THE RECEIVING OF _____. IT LOOKED LIKE
                                  PLURAL NOUN

THEY HAD MORE _____ WATCHING EACH OTHER _____
                   NOUN   VERB

THE _____ THEY HAD CHOSEN FOR EACH OTHER, AND
        PLURAL NOUN

THIS WAS GOOD TO _____. THEY WERE _____ THE
                      VERB   VERB—"ING"

TRUTH OF _____ IN THEIR _____. IT WASN'T
            NAME OF SEASON   PLURAL NOUN

ABOUT _____, IT WAS ABOUT _____.
          VERB—"ING"   VERB—"ING"

93

WHERE ARE THOSE VOWELS?

YOU'RE GOING TO HAVE TO CONCENTRATE FOR THIS ONE! VOWELS ARE HIDDEN IN THE PICTURE BELOW. YOU WILL NEED THEM TO COMPLETE THE PUZZLE.

"B__T THE ANG__L SA__D TO TH__M, 'DO NOT B__ AFRA__D. __ BRING YOU GOOD N__WS OF GR__AT JOY THAT W__LL B__ FOR ALL TH__ P__OPL__. TODAY __N TH__ TOWN OF DAV__D A SAV__OR HAS B__ __N BORN TO YO__; H__ __S CHR__ST TH__ LORD.'"

LUKE 2:10–11

94

JUST A REGULAR OLD CROSSWORD!

ACROSS
1. MOM'S MOM
2. INSIDE A TURKEY
3. OLD STYLE CUP
4. BED FOR JESUS
5. NOT A LONG BREAD

DOWN
1. IN A CHURCH STEEPLE
2. DOWNHILL VEHICLE
3. EASTERN KING
4. TO MOVE ALONG
5. GROUP OF MUSICIANS

95

FIND THE FOUR

COMPLETE THE PUZZLE BELOW BY CROSSING OUT EVERY LETTER THAT APPEARS AT LEAST FOUR TIMES. USE THE REMAINING LETTERS TO COMPLETE THE SENTENCE.

I'LL HAVE THAT BABY *COOKED* IN NO TIME!

MOM'S GOT A BUSY DAY AHEAD, AND RATHER THAN PLAY WITH THEIR NEW TOYS __ __ __ DAY, THE KIDS ARE HELPING TO PREPARE CHRISTMAS DINNER.

it's a Mystery

THIS IS A GREAT GAME TO PLAY AS YOU TRAVEL. YOU'LL NEED SOMEONE TO PLAY IT WITH, THOUGH, LIKE YOUR BROTHER OR SISTER OR FRIENDS.

BELOW IS A LIST OF PHRASES THAT NEED TO BE COMPLETED. SHOW THIS PUZZLE TO EACH PLAYER, WHO PICKS A LETTER TO FILL IN THE BLANKS, AND THEN HAS TEN SECONDS TO GUESS THE PHRASE. MOVE ON TO EACH PLAYER UNTIL THE MYSTERY IS SOLVED! AS THE HOST OF THIS GAME, YOU GET TO CHECK OUT THE SOLUTION FROM THE ANSWER PAGES AT THE BACK (IF YOU NEED TO)!

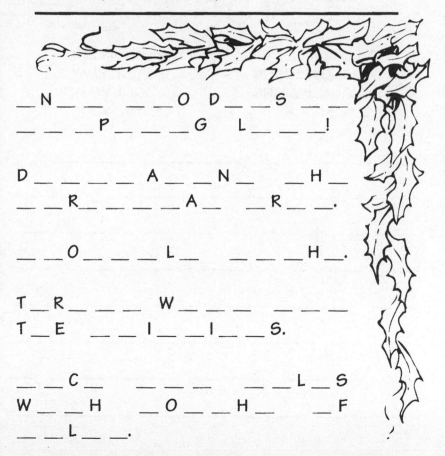

_ N _ _ _   _ _ O   D _ _   S _ _   _ _
_ _   _   P _ _ _   G   L _ _ _ _ !

D _ _ _ _ _   A _ _ N _   _ H _
_ _ R _ _ _ _   _ A _   _ R _   _ .

_ _ O _ _   L _   _ _ _   H _ .

T _ R _ _ _   W _ _ _   _ _ _ _
T _ E   _ _ I _ _ I _ _ S .

_ _ C _ _   _ _ _   _ _ L _ S
W _ _ H   _ O _ _ H _   _ F
_ _ L _ _ .

TRAVELLIN' RHYMES

THIS IS A GREAT GAME TO PLAY AS YOU TRAVEL. YOU'LL NEED SOMEONE TO PLAY IT WITH, THOUGH, LIKE YOUR BROTHER OR SISTER OR FRIENDS.

BELOW IS A LIST OF WORD PAIRS THAT RHYME WITH EACH OTHER. YOUR JOB IS TO CALL OUT THE WORDS AND HAVE THE PLAYERS COME UP WITH THE SILLIEST RHYMES. WRITE THE BEST ON THE SPACES BELOW.

WHOA ...
SEMI-AUTOMATIC!!

DRILL, CHILL   PUFFING, STUFFING
WISHING, FISHING   PRAY, PLAY
SKATING, WAITING   SOCK, WALK
CORN, ADORN   PLANTS, PANTS

_____

_____

_____

_____

_____

_____

_____

_____

DON'T LEAVE IT SCRAMBLED!

UNSCRAMBLE EACH WORD, THEN USE THE CIRCLED LETTERS TO COMPLETE THE PUZZLE BELOW . . . AND I HOPE IT DOESN'T HURT YOUR EYES!

NI   GBLEUMI,   MRSITSAHC   SI

__ _____◯_, _____ __

BTELDAECRE NO TMHRSSIAC VEE,

_____◯____ _____ ___,

IHTW A ELMA FO FOSAEDO NAD

____ A ____ ◯_ _____ ___

YRTKUE. A NARTADLOTII RSDESTE

◯____. _ _____ _____

SI A ECKA MDEA IHWT MCEAR,

__ _ ◯___ ____ ____ _____,

LDLEAC A CRSMATISH GLO.

_____ _ _____ ___◯.

SNSPRETE REA NEPDOE YAREL,

_____ ___ ◯____ _____,

NO CRBDMEEE TXSIH!

__ _____ _____!

A SPECIAL SWEET BREAD FOR BREAKFAST IS CALLED

◯ ◯ ◯ ◯ ◯ ◯ ◯ .

99

PICTURE MAKER

YOU MAKE THE PICTURE. DRAW THE IMAGE FROM EACH FRAME AT THE TOP IN THE FRAME BELOW WITH THE MATCHING NUMBER.

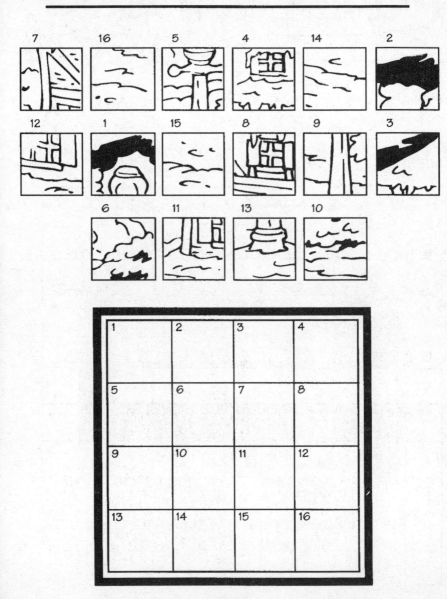

UP OR DOWN?

UNSCRAMBLE THE WORDS, THEN IT'S UP TO YOU TO FIND WHERE EACH WORD GOES. WE PUT A FEW LETTERS IN TO HELP.

LCOSHANI _____   UCEL _____
EUMIGLB _____   ESSTRDE _____
PRFIEECLA _____   RWCNO _____
GCKNITSOS _____   ETFAHR _____
MEDEER _____   EGTA _____

"ZALIG KERSTFEET" MEANS MERRY CHRISTMAS IN BELGIUM!

FIND THE FOUR

COMPLETE THE PUZZLE BELOW BY CROSSING OUT EVERY LETTER THAT APPEARS AT LEAST FOUR TIMES. USE THE REMAINING LETTERS TO COMPLETE THE SENTENCE.

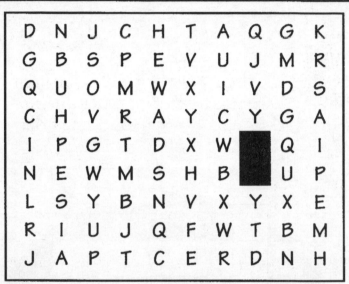

```
D  N  J  C  H  T  A  Q  G  K
G  B  S  P  E  V  U  J  M  R
Q  U  O  M  W  X  I  V  D  S
C  H  V  R  A  Y  C  Y  G  A
I  P  G  T  D  X  W     Q  I
N  E  W  M  S  H  B     U  P
L  S  Y  B  N  V  X  Y  X  E
R  I  U  J  Q  F  W  T  B  M
J  A  P  T  C  E  R  D  N  H
```

THAT'S SOME COSTUME.

YOU'RE ONE TA' TALK ...!

IN BRAZIL, THEY ENJOY _ _ _ _ PLAYS AT CHRISTMAS.

CAN YOU FIND THE WORDS?

ALL THESE
WORDS ARE HIDDEN IN
THE PUZZLE BELOW.
HAVE FUN!

FESTIVAL
PAGEANT
SINGING
ORCHIDS
CUSTOMS

DANCING
PLAYS
FANDANGO
ORNAMENTS
DANCE

```
K C Q S B R        L B F J L
J Y P A G E A N T P Q P H T
S N D N H F E S T I V A L
  I A F O R N A M E N T S
  F N K A J D N C W D G
  P C G S N M B V T V O N
  L I C I K D W N Q E R C P
P A N Q H N R A H C G C K
G Y G L F V G T N V L H F
B S N M N E P A K G R I
P D R V A T D J L S O D N
  T W Q C U S T O M S R
  J C W L     M D T Y W
  G S H           F M B X
```

103

LET'S MAZE AROUND

TRAVEL THROUGH SOUTH AMERICA TO GET TO BRAZIL.

ALL JUMBLED UP

HEY . . . THIS ONE WILL BE FUN!
FIND THE OPPOSITE OF EACH WORD,
THEN USE THE CIRCLED LETTERS TO
COMPLETE THE PUZZLE BELOW.

MERRY   ◯ _ _

DINNER   _ _ ◯ _ ◯ _ _ _

SOUTH   ◯◯ _ _ _

RECORDED   _ _ _ ◯ _

STRAIGHT   _ _ _ - ◯ _ _

SLEEP   ◯ _ _ _ _

RUN   _ _ ◯ _

IN BRAZIL, "B ◯◯ S   F ◯ STA ◯

E ◯ E ◯ I ◯ ANO ◯ O ◯ O ,"

MEANS HAPPY HOLIDAYS.

105

WHERE ARE THOSE VOWELS?

YOU'RE GOING TO HAVE TO CONCENTRATE FOR THIS ONE! VOWELS ARE HIDDEN IN THE PICTURE BELOW. YOU WILL NEED THEM TO COMPLETE THE PUZZLE.

B _ X _ NG D _ Y _ S THE B _ G
CHR _ STM _ S CELEBR _ T _ _ N
_ N ENGL _ ND _ ND _ S _
N _ T _ _ N _ L H _ L _ D _ Y. B _ XED
PRESENTS, PL _ CED _ N CHURCHES
THR _ UGH _ UT THE YE _ R, _ RE
_ PENED _ N TH _ S D _ Y.

LESS SHALL BE FIRST

PLACE THE WORDS BELOW INTO THE PUZZLE ACCORDING TO THE NUMBER OF LETTERS IN EACH WORD, BEGINNING WITH THE WORD THAT HAS THE FEWEST LETTERS. THEN, UNSCRAMBLE THE CIRCLED LETTERS TO COMPLETE THE ANSWER BELOW.

HOLIDAY   NATIONAL
PRINCIPLE   ACTS
BOXED   STONED
LED

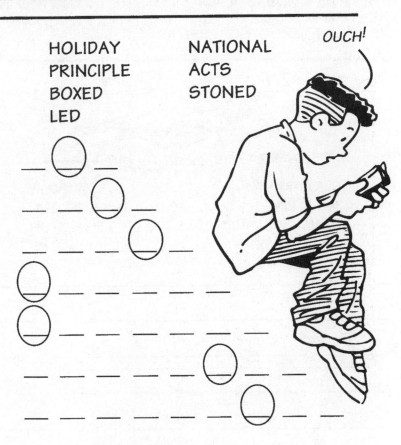

THIS DAY IS ALSO CALLED

SAINT ⃝ ⃝ ⃝ ⃝ ⃝ ⃝ ⃝ DAY,
AFTER THE CHRISTIAN MARTYR WHO WAS STONED TO DEATH, AS TOLD IN THE BOOK OF ACTS.

TRAVELLIN' RHYMES

THIS IS A GREAT GAME TO PLAY AS YOU TRAVEL. YOU'LL NEED SOMEONE TO PLAY IT WITH, THOUGH, LIKE YOUR BROTHER OR SISTER OR FRIENDS.

BELOW IS A LIST OF WORD PAIRS THAT RHYME WITH EACH OTHER. YOUR JOB IS TO CALL OUT THE WORDS AND HAVE THE PLAYERS COME UP WITH THE SILLIEST RHYMES. WRITE THE BEST ON THE SPACES BELOW.

PLAY, GRAY   SNOW, FLOW
SING, RING   TOWN, BROWN
DANCE, GLANCE   FISH, DISH
GREEN, SCREEN   BOX, WALKS

_____

_____

_____

_____

_____

_____

_____

COMPLETE THE PUZZLE BELOW BY CROSSING OUT EVERY LETTER THAT APPEARS AT LEAST FOUR TIMES. USE THE REMAINING LETTERS TO COMPLETE THE SENTENCE.

SO . . . THIS IS YOUR GREAT IDEA?!

E	N	I	D	J	S	B	F	G	A
M	K	Q	U	G	P	W	V	M	Q
C	F	W	X	A	Q	D	S		I
O	J	X	L	U	M	J	H		B
G	V	B	H	N	T	K	W	L	X
S	P	U	C	O	I	G	A	O	V
A	N	D	J	Q	F	W	P	V	D
H	K	M	X	R	S	C	L	U	F
L	C	P	H	O	B	K	N	I	E

LEGEND TELLS US THAT IT WAS IN GERMANY WHERE THE CHRISTMAS __ __ __ __ WAS SUPPOSEDLY FIRST INTRODUCED.

PICTURE MAKER

YOU MAKE THE PICTURE. DRAW THE IMAGE FROM EACH FRAME AT THE TOP IN THE FRAME BELOW WITH THE MATCHING NUMBER.

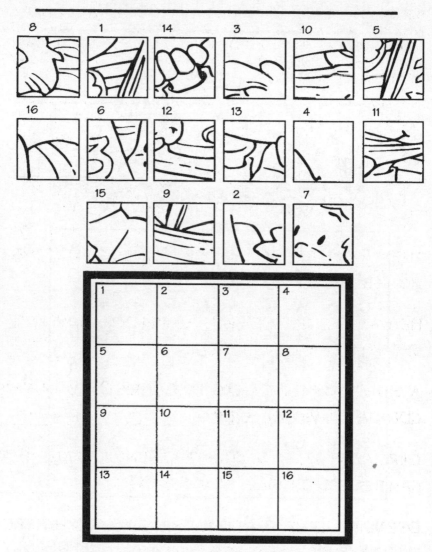

CHRISTMAS BEGINS EARLY IN GERMANY WITH THE ANNUAL TOY FAIR, OR "CHRISTKINDLESMARKT."

WHO, WHAT, WHERE

THIS IS A GREAT GAME TO PLAY AS YOU TRAVEL. YOU'LL NEED SOMEONE TO PLAY IT WITH, THOUGH, LIKE YOUR BROTHER OR SISTER OR FRIENDS.

BELOW IS A LIST OF QUESTIONS THAT NEED A "WHO, WHAT, OR WHERE" ANSWER. EACH PLAYER HAS TEN SECONDS TO ANSWER. AS THE HOST OF THIS GAME, YOU GET TO CHECK OUT THE SOLUTION FROM THE ANSWER PAGES AT THE BACK (IF YOU NEED TO)!

THEY FIRST BEGAN TO BRING THESE INTO THEIR HOMES. *WHAT* IS IT? _____

HE WAS THE ONE BEHIND THE REFORMATION AND A CHRISTMAS SYMBOL. *WHO* IS HE? _____

A HUGE TOY FAIR KICKS OFF CHRISTMAS IN THIS COUNTRY. *WHERE* IS IT? _____

GERMANS LOVE TO DECORATE AROUND A FRAME THAT CAN BE SEEN OUTSIDE. *WHAT* IS IT? _____

GERMANS LOVE TO HEAR THIS GROUP WHO VISIT THEIR HOMES. *WHO* ARE THEY? _____

IT'S A MYSTERY

THIS IS A GREAT GAME TO PLAY AS YOU TRAVEL. YOU'LL NEED SOMEONE TO PLAY IT WITH, THOUGH, LIKE YOUR BROTHER OR SISTER OR FRIENDS.

BELOW IS A LIST OF PHRASES THAT NEED TO BE COMPLETED. SHOW THIS PUZZLE TO EACH PLAYER, WHO PICKS A LETTER TO FILL IN THE BLANKS, AND THEN HAS TEN SECONDS TO GUESS THE PHRASE. MOVE ON TO EACH PLAYER UNTIL THE MYSTERY IS SOLVED! AS THE HOST OF THIS GAME, YOU GET TO CHECK OUT THE SOLUTION FROM THE ANSWER PAGES AT THE BACK (IF YOU NEED TO)!

O __ A __ __ __ __ B __ __ M.

__ __ E __ D __ E __ __ __ __ __ __ E __ __ A __
__ __ __ A __ __ __ __ D __ __ IO __ __ I __
__ __ R __ A __ __.

IN G __ __ __ A __ Y, __ O __ __ L __ __
TR __ __ TS __ RE FI __ __ R __ S __ __ D __
__ F S __ __ AR __ M __ __ Z __ P __ N
D __ __ G __.

__ __ S __ Y M __ __ R __ __ H __ __ ST __ A __
I __ __ __ RM __ N __ __ U __ D B __,
"FR __ EC __ __ ICH __ __ EIN __ AC __ __ EN."

F __ R C __ __ L __ __ EN, __ TO __
__ __ I __ I __ __ __ E B __ __ T WA __
TO __ E __ __ __ CH __ __ S __ M __ S.

112

JUST A REGULAR OLD CROSSWORD!

ACROSS

1. FUN CELEBRATION
2. SEASONAL EVENT
3. A PERFORMANCE
4. COLOR OF RIBBON
5. BRINGS LIGHT

DOWN

1. SWEDISH PROCESSIONS
2. COUNTRY OF BLONDS
3. DECORATIVE LIGHT
4. DRESSLIKE GARMENT
5. VERY SHORT IN DECEMBER

WHO, WHAT, WHERE

THIS IS A GREAT GAME TO PLAY AS YOU TRAVEL. YOU'LL NEED SOMEONE TO PLAY IT WITH, THOUGH, LIKE YOUR BROTHER OR SISTER OR FRIENDS.

BELOW IS A LIST OF QUESTIONS THAT NEED A "WHO, WHAT, OR WHERE" ANSWER. EACH PLAYER HAS TEN SECONDS TO ANSWER. AS THE HOST OF THIS GAME, YOU GET TO CHECK OUT THE SOLUTION FROM THE ANSWER PAGES AT THE BACK (IF YOU NEED TO)!

IN THIS COUNTRY, THE SHORTEST, DARKEST DAY IS DECEMBER 22. *WHERE* IS IT? _____

A SPECIAL MEAL IS EATEN ON THIS MOST IMPORTANT DAY. *WHAT* DAY IS IT? _____

IN SWEDEN, MANY GO HERE TO MEET ON CHRISTMAS MORNING. *WHERE* IS IT? _____

BECAUSE OF WINTER DARKNESS, THESE ARE VERY IMPORTANT. *WHAT* ARE THEY? _____

KRINGLE, KRUMKAKE, AND SANDBAKKELS ARE TRADITIONAL. *WHAT* ARE THEY? _____

AN IMPORTANT FIGURE IN SWEDISH TRADITION WHO WAS MARTYRED. *WHO* IS SHE? _____

IN SWEDEN, THE TRADITIONAL CHRISTMAS GREETING IS, "GOD JUL."

PICTURE MAKER

YOU MAKE THE PICTURE. DRAW THE IMAGE FROM EACH FRAME AT THE TOP IN THE FRAME BELOW WITH THE MATCHING NUMBER.

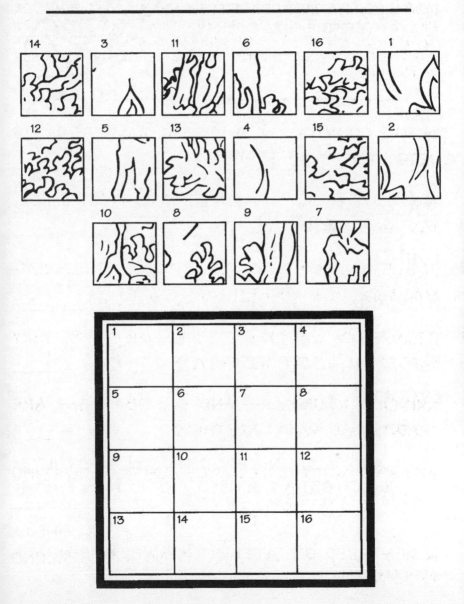

ALL JUMBLED UP

HEY . . . THIS ONE WILL BE FUN!
FIND THE OPPOSITE OF EACH WORD,
THEN USE THE CIRCLED LETTERS TO
COMPLETE THE PUZZLE BELOW.

BELIEF _ _ (_) _ _

NIGHT _ (_) _

BLACK _ _ (_) _ _

YOUNG (_) _ _

FORWARD _ _ (_) _ _ _ _

SIT _ (_) _ _

CROOKED (_) _ _ _ _ _ _ _

LONG AGO, A YOUNG SWEDISH GIRL WAS KILLED
FOR HER CHRISTIAN BELIEFS AND IS NOW KNOWN

AS (_) (_) . (_) (_) (_) (_) (_). SHE IS
REMEMBERED ON DECEMBER 13, WHICH IS NOW A
SPECIAL DAY IN THE SWEDISH CHRISTMAS.

116

CAN YOU FIND THE WORDS?

ALL THESE
WORDS ARE HIDDEN IN
THE PUZZLE BELOW.
HAVE FUN!

ST. LUCIA   HOLIDAY
CROWN   DRESS
SWEDEN   BEADS
GINGERBREAD   ROBE
LIGHT   RIBBON
BREAD   GARLAND

```
        B L E J
      D G B F L N
      K O L G Q P
      R H P I M K
F C R I B B O N G D R E S S
H S R H M P G G D H F J M G
C K T . O J C M E N B T P B L
      L W F N R H Q N
      I U N B B J E K
    I D L C K R D L B I
    D A H G I E E D E H
    G Y B J W A C A A K
    T C D S E D H F D H
  G A R L A N D B G S C W
```

LETTER CLUES

TO DECODE THIS MESSAGE, YOU'LL NEED TO TAKE THE LETTER FROM EACH NUMBERED CLUE AND MATCH IT TO THE NUMBERED SPACE IN THE PUZZLE BELOW.

_____

1. THIS LETTER IS FOUND IN BOTH *DRESS* AND *GET*.
    _____

2. IT'S FOUND ONCE IN *ROBE* AND TWICE IN *RIBBON*.
    _____

3. FOUND FIRST IN BOTH *CANDLES* AND IN *CANDY*.
    _____

4. FOUND FIRST IN BOTH *FRANCE* AND IN *FRENCH*.
    _____

5. THIS LETTER BEGINS *X-RAY* AND ENDS *BOX*.
    _____

6. THIS LETTER IS FOUND IN *REST* BUT NOT IN *BEST*.
    _____

IN _ _ AN _ _ , _ H _ ISTMAS T _ _ _ S
   4 6   3 1   3   6   6 1 1

A _ _   D _ _ O _ AT _ D   WITH   WHIT _
 6 1   1 3 6   1   1

_ ANDL _ S AND _ _ D _ I _ _ ONS. _ V _ N
3   1   6 1   6 2 2   1   1

T _ _ _ S OUTSID _   A _ _   D _ _ O _ AT _ D
 6 1 1   1   6 1   1 3 6   1

AND LIT TH _ OUGH TH _   NIGHT. IN TH _
           6   1   1

LANGUAG _   OF TH _   _ _ _ N _ H, ON _
        1   1   4 6 1 3   1

WOULD H _ A _ M _ _ _ Y _ H _ ISTMAS AS,
       1   6   1 6 6   3   6

"JOY _ U _   NO _ L."
     1   5   1

118

LESS SHALL BE FIRST

PLACE THE WORDS BELOW INTO THE PUZZLE ACCORDING TO THE NUMBER OF LETTERS IN EACH WORD, BEGINNING WITH THE WORD THAT HAS THE FEWEST LETTERS. THEN, UNSCRAMBLE THE CIRCLED LETTERS TO COMPLETE THE ANSWER BELOW.

HOLIDAY   BOW

ROBE   BEAUTIFUL

PICTURES   WINDOW

BREAD

CANDLES AND ◯ ◯ ◯ ◯ ◯ ◯ ◯ _ _ _ _ _ _ _

ARE A PART OF A FRENCH CHRISTMAS.

119

DON'T LEAVE IT SCRAMBLED!

UNSCRAMBLE EACH WORD, THEN USE THE CIRCLED LETTERS TO COMPLETE THE PUZZLE BELOW . . . AND I HOPE IT DOESN'T HURT YOUR EYES!

OESTH NI NADII HOW EAR FO

_ _ _ _ _   _ _   _ _ _ _ _   _ _ _   _ _ _   _ _

HET THRNSIAIC TAHIF TECLERBAE

_ _ _   _ _ _ _ _ _ _ _ _   _ _ _ _ _   _ _ _ _ _ _ _ _

AITHMSSCR SA LELW. TYEH

_ _ _ _ _ _ _ _ _   _ _   _ _ _ _.   _ _ _ _

OTREDECA HREIT HHCRUSCE IHWT

_ _ _ _ _ _ _ _   _ _ _ _ _   _ _ _ _ _ _ _ _   _ _ _ _

A TBFLUEUIA WLFEOR ELALCD

_   _ _ _ _ _ _ _ _ _   _ _ _ _ _ _   _ _ _ _ _ _

HTE EITAPOSTIN NAD AGONM RO

_ _ _   _ _ _ _ _ _ _ _ _   _ _ _   _ _ _ _ _   _ _

BNAANA ESRET RAE LLUFOYLRCO

_ _ _ _ _ _   _ _ _ _ _   _ _ _   _ _ _ _ _ _ _ _ _

RTDNONEMEA.

_ _ _ _ _ _ _ _ _ _.

IN INDIA, ◯ ◯ ◯ ◯ ◯ ◯ ◯ IS CALLED, "BAKSHEESH."

LET'S MAZE AROUND

SOME CHRISTIANS IN INDIA DECORATE THEIR HOMES WITH SMALL CLAY LAMPS. MAKE YOUR WAY THROUGH THE STREETS TO GET HOME IN TIME FOR THE CELEBRATION.

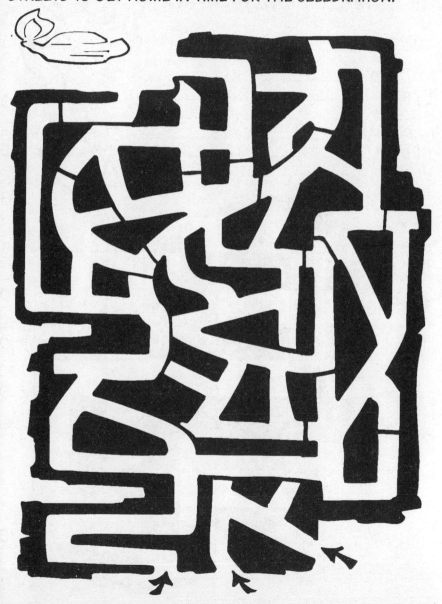

UP OR DOWN?

UNSCRAMBLE THE WORDS, THEN IT'S UP TO YOU TO FIND WHERE EACH WORD GOES. WE PUT A FEW LETTERS IN TO HELP.

FPTOORO   _____   OYJ   _____

TSNPEOAIIT   _____   DNAII   _____

IASTELFV   _____   ISFTG   _____

NHDGTIMI   _____   SAMS   _____

YRHACTI   _____   WLLA   _____

MIYFLA   _____   TPO   _____

WHERE ARE THOSE VOWELS?

YOU'RE GOING TO HAVE TO CONCENTRATE FOR THIS ONE! VOWELS ARE HIDDEN IN THE PICTURE BELOW. YOU WILL NEED THEM TO COMPLETE THE PUZZLE.

IN FINL_ND, CHRISTM_S EVE, CHRISTM_S D_Y, _ND B_XING D__Y _RE HELD T_ BE THE THREE H_LY D_YS. CHRISTM__S DINNER IS C_NSIDERED _ FE_ST _FTER _ LIGHT BRE_KF_ST _F PL_M J_ICE _ND RICE P__RRIDGE.

PICTURE CLUES

THE PICTURES ARE YOUR ONLY CLUES TO COMPLETING THIS CROSSWORD. THIS IS A BIT OF A BRAIN TEASER.

FIND THE FOUR

COMPLETE THE PUZZLE BELOW BY CROSSING OUT EVERY LETTER THAT APPEARS AT LEAST FOUR TIMES. USE THE REMAINING LETTERS TO COMPLETE THE SENTENCE.

I CAN'T *READ* IT . . . MUCH LESS SAY IT!

```
D  Q  I  F  C  V  J  M  Q  A
N  L  U  G  P  D  X  B  Y  V
K  B  V  E  M  Y  W  Z  T  J
S  R  Y  K  J  A  Z  F  G  M
G  N  C  Z  [      ]  C  D  X
P  W  L  D  N  Z  H  U  P  W
E  U  X  F  Y  E  L  X  K  F
M  A  S  U  O  G  A  V  B  Q
J  Q  B  W  N  K  P  E  L  C
```

THE CHRISTMAS GREETING IN RUSSIA IS

" _ _ _ _ _ _ _ RAZDAJETSJA."

125

it's a Mystery

THIS IS A GREAT GAME TO PLAY AS YOU TRAVEL. YOU'LL NEED SOMEONE TO PLAY IT WITH, THOUGH, LIKE YOUR BROTHER OR SISTER OR FRIENDS.

BELOW IS A LIST OF PHRASES THAT NEED TO BE COMPLETED. SHOW THIS PUZZLE TO EACH PLAYER, WHO PICKS A LETTER TO FILL IN THE BLANKS, AND THEN HAS TEN SECONDS TO GUESS THE PHRASE. MOVE ON TO EACH PLAYER UNTIL THE MYSTERY IS SOLVED! AS THE HOST OF THIS GAME, YOU GET TO CHECK OUT THE SOLUTION FROM THE ANSWER PAGES AT THE BACK (IF YOU NEED TO)!

T _ _   C _ _ L _ PS _   O _   T _ E
_ OV _ _ T   U _ I _ _.

_ H _   R _ _ SI _ N   P _ O _ _ _   A _ E
F _ E _   _ _   _ E _ _ B _ A _ _
C _ _ IS _ MA _.

CH _ I _ _ MA _   _ N _ US _ I _   I _
_ E _ _ BR _ TE _   _ _ R   TW _ L _ _ _
D _ _ S, _ R _ M   D _ _ EM _ _ R   25
_ _   _ A _ _ AR _   5.

_ _ SS _ AN   CE _ E _ _ ATI _ N _
I _ CL _ D _   _ _ R _ U _ _ S,
S _ O _ _ S, A _ _   _ _ _ NIV _ LS.

126

PICTURE MAKER

YOU MAKE THE PICTURE. DRAW THE IMAGE FROM EACH FRAME AT THE TOP IN THE FRAME BELOW WITH THE MATCHING NUMBER.

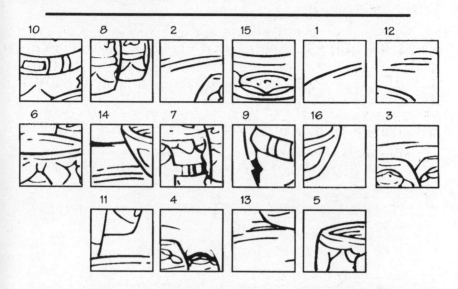

MATRYOSHKU DOLLS, A TRADITIONAL RUSSIAN PRESENT.

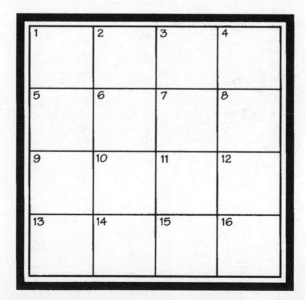

LETTER CLUES

TO DECODE THIS MESSAGE, YOU'LL NEED TO TAKE THE LETTER FROM EACH NUMBERED CLUE AND MATCH IT TO THE NUMBERED SPACE IN THE PUZZLE BELOW.

1. THIS LETTER BEGINS BOTH *HEAR* AND *HERE*.
   _____

2. THIS LETTER ENDS BOTH *BLOCK* AND *BLACK*.
   _____

3. THIS LETTER IS FOUND IN *CAST* BUT NOT IN *LAST*.
   _____

4. IT ENDS THE WORD *CAT* AND BEGINS THE WORD *TOY*.
   _____

5. IT APPEARS TWICE IN *SOON* AND ONCE IN *HOT*.
   _____

6. IT'S FOUND ONCE IN *FIVE* AND TWICE IN *VALVE*.
   _____

7. THIS LETTER IS FOUND IN *GIFT* BUT NOT IN *RIFT*.
   _____

8. THIS LETTER BEGINS BOTH *BLOCK* AND *BLACK*.
   _____

_ _ R I S _ I A N S   I N   _ _ N _   _ _ N _
3 1   4   1 5 7   2 5 7

_ A _ E   A D A P _ E D   _ _ E   _ _ R I S _ M A S
1 6   4   4 1   3 1   4

_ E L E _ R A _ I _ N   I N _ _   A N   E A S _ E R N
3   8   4 5   4 5   4

S E _ _ I N _.   N A _ I _ I _ Y   S _ E N E S   A N D
  4 4   7   4 6 4   3

_ _ R I S _ M A S   _ A R D S   _ A _ E   A
3 1   4   3   1 6

_ _ I N E S E   L _ _ _   A N D   A R E   _ E R Y
3 1   5 5 2   6

A R _ I S _ I _.
  4   4 3

128

CAN YOU FIND THE WORDS?

ALL THESE WORDS ARE HIDDEN IN THE PUZZLE BELOW. HAVE FUN!

HONG
KONG
CHINESE
EASTERN

STREAMER
CARDS
LAMPS
NATIVITY

```
    G P C L H O N G Y N
      C T M S K O N G J R F
      H V B W D S K Y
      N I R F P Q T N
    J D Q F N M Z L G A W J
  H C S G K A E Y R S T B K
    A Z L T P S B R I
    V R J N W Q E M V
V B D T F D K H M A D I N G
L G P C Y T S A R S F T F P
    F Q W H E M L T B Y S
    B K R F N T E Z K V
  Z L S T K Q D P R W B F C
  C J M S R H V C F N H Y M K
```

129

JUST A REGULAR OLD CROSSWORD!

ACROSS

1. RETURNED TO CHINA
2. EASTERN LANGUAGE
3. PLACES OF WORSHIP

DOWN

1. CHINESE WORD PICTURE
2. CHINESE PAPER ORNAMENT
3. LONG PAPER DECORATION

PICTURE CLUES

THE PICTURES ARE YOUR ONLY CLUES TO COMPLETING THIS CROSSWORD. THIS IS A BIT OF A BRAIN TEASER.

ALL JUMBLED UP

HEY . . . THIS ONE WILL BE FUN!
FIND THE OPPOSITE OF EACH WORD,
THEN USE THE CIRCLED LETTERS TO
COMPLETE THE PUZZLE BELOW.

WEST _ ◯ _ _

WATER _ _ ◯ _ _

SHOES _ _ _ ◯ _ _ _ _ _

ADULT ◯ _ _ _ _ _

SOFT _ ◯ _ _

CAN YOU PRONOUNCE THE CHRISTMAS GEETING IN

◯ ◯ ◯ ◯ ◯
_ _ _ _ _ : "SHINNEN

OMEDETO, KURISUMASU OMEDETO"? *WOW!*

132

FIND THE FOUR

COMPLETE THE PUZZLE BELOW BY CROSSING OUT EVERY LETTER THAT APPEARS AT LEAST FOUR TIMES. USE THE REMAINING LETTERS TO COMPLETE THE SENTENCE.

D	R	W	A	R	K	Z	V	A	J
J	T	X	Z	J	W	T	P	I	X
L	D	V	Y	D	G	F	S	K	H
Q	M	F	X	Q	S	U	C	T	Y
E	S	W	L	C	H	R	G	E	R
H	P	J	I	P	Q	A	I	N	M
A	V	M	M	L	X	Y	V	M	Q
K	B	C	E	W	S	F	Z	D	S
G	I	K	H	E	Z	P	Y	R	M
F	G	Y	T	C	L	O	J	H	A

ITALIAN CUSTOMS? THEY'RE THE GREATEST!

" _ _ _ _ NATALE" IS HOW YOU SAY MERRY CHRISTMAS IN ITALY.

133

WHO, WHAT, WHERE

THIS IS A GREAT GAME TO PLAY AS YOU TRAVEL. YOU'LL NEED SOMEONE TO PLAY IT WITH, THOUGH, LIKE YOUR BROTHER OR SISTER OR FRIENDS.

BELOW IS A LIST OF QUESTIONS THAT NEED A "WHO, WHAT, OR WHERE" ANSWER. EACH PLAYER HAS TEN SECONDS TO ANSWER. AS THE HOST OF THIS GAME, YOU GET TO CHECK OUT THE SOLUTION FROM THE ANSWER PAGES AT THE BACK (IF YOU NEED TO)!

CHILDREN HOPE THAT "GESÚ BAMBINO" WILL BRING THEM GIFTS. *WHO* IS HE? _____

"PRESEPIO" IS AN ITALIAN NAME FOR A FAMILIAR CHRISTMAS SCENE. *WHAT* IS IT? _____

THESE ARE SPECIAL "BAGS" THAT MEN MAKE MUSIC ON. *WHAT* ARE THEY?

_____

IN ITALY, ONLY THIS MEAT IS EATEN ON THE FAST AT CHRISTMAS EVE. *WHAT* IS IT? _____

NO ITALIAN MEAL CAN BE COMPLETE WITHOUT THIS TRADITIONAL DISH. *WHAT* IS IT? _____

MUSICIANS DRESS IN SHEEPSKIN JACKETS AS A REMINDER OF THESE WHO WERE PRESENT AT CHRIST'S BIRTH. *WHO* ARE THEY? _____

LET'S MAZE AROUND

HELP THE MUSICIANS FIND THEIR WAY TO THE CHRISTMAS FEAST.

TRAVELLIN' RHYMES

THIS IS A GREAT GAME TO PLAY AS YOU TRAVEL. YOU'LL NEED SOMEONE TO PLAY IT WITH, THOUGH, LIKE YOUR BROTHER OR SISTER OR FRIENDS.

BELOW IS A LIST OF WORD PAIRS THAT RHYME WITH EACH OTHER. YOUR JOB IS TO CALL OUT THE WORDS AND HAVE THE PLAYERS COME UP WITH THE SILLIEST RHYMES. WRITE THE BEST ON THE SPACES BELOW.

FISH, DISH   HEAR, MIRROR
STREET, MEAT   FAST, PAST
JOY, TOY   DAY, PLAY
LIGHT, BRIGHT   EIGHT, ATE
JUICE, LOOSE   SPEED, FEED

_____

_____

_____

_____

_____

_____

_____

_____

_____

DON'T LEAVE IT SCRAMBLED!

UNSCRAMBLE EACH WORD, THEN USE THE CIRCLED LETTERS TO COMPLETE THE PUZZLE BELOW . . . AND I HOPE IT DOESN'T HURT YOUR EYES!

NI PINAS, THMSSCRIA EEV SI

__ _____, _____ ___ __

OLAS ONWNK SA ETH GTNIH FO

(_)_ _____ __ ___ _____ __

DOGO ITDIGNS. A IILNARDATTO

____ _____. _ (_)_____

MAGE SI EON HEWER DRIHCELN

____ __ (_)__ _____ _____

HTI TA A RETE RNUKT LFLU

___ __ _ ____ (_)____ ____

FO IOODGSE, IRNGTY OT ONCKK

__ _____(_)_, _____ (_) _____

ETMH UTO.

____ (_)__.

SPAIN HAS A LEGEND OF A COAL MINER, NAMED

(_)(_)(_)(_)(_) Z (_)(_)(_), WHO

CAME DOWN FROM A MOUNTAIN TO ANNOUNCE THE BIRTH OF CHRIST.

PICTURE MAKER

YOU MAKE THE PICTURE. DRAW THE IMAGE FROM EACH FRAME AT THE TOP IN THE FRAME BELOW WITH THE MATCHING NUMBER.

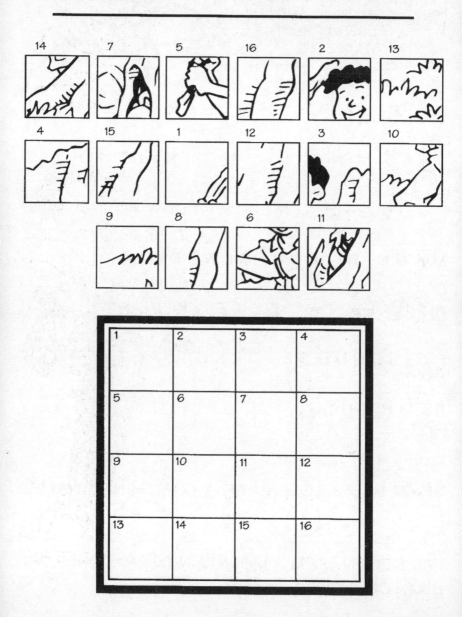

ALL JUMBLED UP

HEY . . . THIS ONE WILL BE FUN!
FIND THE OPPOSITE OF EACH WORD,
THEN USE THE CIRCLED LETTERS TO
COMPLETE THE PUZZLE BELOW.

LATE ◯ _ _ _ _

WARM _ _ ◯ _ _

MESSY _ ◯ _ _

QUIET ◯ _ _ _

BACK ◯ _ _ _

HOT ◯ _ _ _

SLOW _ _ ◯ _

"◯ ◯ ◯ ◯ ◯ ◯ ◯ PASCUAS"

MEANS MERRY CHRISTMAS IN SPAIN.

139

WHERE ARE THOSE VOWELS?

YOU'RE GOING TO HAVE TO CONCENTRATE FOR THIS ONE! VOWELS ARE HIDDEN IN THE PICTURE BELOW. YOU WILL NEED THEM TO COMPLETE THE PUZZLE.

__N MEX__C__, THE N__NE DAYS BEF__RE CHR__STMAS ARE KN__WN AS THE P__SADA, WHERE__N, EVERY N__GHT, FAM__L__ES AND FR__ENDS J____N T__GETHER T__ F__ND A REF__GE F__R THE BABY JES__S. THEY HAVE A B__G PARTY __N THE LAST N__GHT, WHEN A REF__GE __S F____ND.

CAN YOU FIND THE WORDS?

ALL THESE WORDS ARE HIDDEN IN THE PUZZLE BELOW. *HAVE FUN!*

FRIENDS
FAMILY
PINATA
FEAST
MEXICO

REFUGE
POSADA
SEARCH
MARIACHI
HORN

```
    J S              N T K
  C P S K G F H S V B F      N C
    N E D Q M A R I A C H I V
      A R Z E E M P S T R J F
      F R K F G W X I K H A M
  G L C X U T M F K L D W L
  W M H F R S Z L Q A Y D Z
  H X E B L D G T S B H X N T
  Q R P X K S K O D G J O C S
    M K J I V P R N D H L R V
    T C T Z C W P E Z M W P N
      M B N O P I N A T A D
      R Q X K C R J V F Q
      B G     S F H B T L
```

UP OR DOWN?

UNSCRAMBLE THE WORDS, THEN IT'S UP TO YOU TO FIND WHERE EACH WORD GOES. WE PUT A FEW LETTERS IN TO HELP.

SDAOPA _____

RELCETAOBNI

_____

DANYC _____

GFUERE _____

NTAAIP _____

EUSSJ _____

EPSI _____

TNSU _____

THE CHRISTMAS GREETING IN MEXICO IS, "FELIZ NAVIDAD."

142

CAN YOU FIND THE WORDS?

ALL THESE WORDS ARE HIDDEN IN THE PUZZLE BELOW. *HAVE FUN!*

CANDY
TOYS
TREASURE
STICK
PARTY

NINE
BIBLICAL
POTTERY
HORSE
CHILDREN

```
            P F X
      H N I N E                    J
      P O T T E R Y            B G
   L N H C B P G D N F    L S
   B J R M C R A V H K Y
   S F T K H J B R M O S        T
      T R G I P I L T W R Q C
H  E R L C B Q S Y V S K
Q C C A N D Y L T C L P N E
T M V S H R Q I F H J R K X
   K Z U W E N C V D W C G
   P D R H N P A B T I S D
   N E L S K L R T H L Z
      M B F Q D S G M J
```

143

LETTER CLUES

TO DECODE THIS MESSAGE, YOU'LL NEED TO TAKE THE LETTER FROM EACH NUMBERED CLUE AND MATCH IT TO THE NUMBERED SPACE IN THE PUZZLE BELOW.

---

1. THIS LETTER IS FOUND IN *SAND* BUT NOT IN *LAND*.

    _____

2. IT APPEARS ONCE IN *BALL* AND TWICE IN *PASTA*.

    _____

3. THIS LETTER BEGINS THE WORD *LORD* AND *LANE*.

    _____

4. IT'S FOUND IN *FATTER* BUT NOT IN *MATTER*.

    _____

5. THIS LETTER IS FOUND IN *YARN* BUT NOT IN *BARN*.

    _____

```
_ _THOUGH THE_ DO NOT CE_EBR_TE
2 3          5            3    2
CHRI_TM_ _ IN I_R_E_, THE_ DO
     1   2 1    1 2  3    5
H_VE _N IMPORT_NT HO_ID_ _ _T
 2   2        2      3  2 5 2
THI_ TIME O_ THE _E_R. IT I_
   1      2      3  2       1
C_ _ _ED, "H_NUKK_H", _ND IT I_
 2 3 3      4     5    2        1
_ _ _O KNOWN _ _ THE _E_TIV_ _
2 3 1        2 1     4  1   2 3
O_ _IGHT_ _ND I_ REPRE_ENTED B_
 4 3     3    2         1        5
_N EIGHT-BR_NCH MENOR_H, OR
2          1         5
C_ND_E HO_DER. IT CE_EBR_TE_ _
 2  3    3        3    2    1 2
MIR_C_E O_ _ONG _GO WHEN THE
   2 3   3  4  3    2
OI_, ON_ _ ENOUGH TO BURN _OR
  3    3 5                4
ONE D_ _ IN _ _ _MP, _ _ _TED
     2 5   2   3 2    3 2 1
_OR EIGHT D_ _ _!
4          2 5 1
```

144

LESS SHALL BE FIRST

PLACE THE WORDS BELOW INTO THE PUZZLE ACCORDING TO THE NUMBER OF LETTERS IN EACH WORD, BEGINNING WITH THE WORD THAT HAS THE FEWEST LETTERS. THEN, UNSCRAMBLE THE CIRCLED LETTERS TO COMPLETE THE ANSWER BELOW.

CHRISTMAS   EIGHT

LIGHTS   HISTORICAL

HANUKKAH   MENORAH

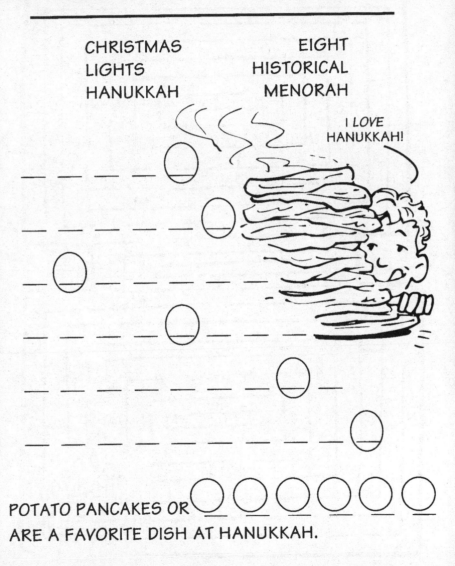

I LOVE HANUKKAH!

POTATO PANCAKES OR ○ ○ ○ ○ ○ ○

ARE A FAVORITE DISH AT HANUKKAH.

LET'S MAZE AROUND

GET THROUGH THE TEMPLE TO LIGHT THE MENORAH FOR HANUKKAH.

FIND THE FOUR

COMPLETE THE PUZZLE BELOW BY CROSSING OUT EVERY LETTER THAT APPEARS AT LEAST FOUR TIMES. USE THE REMAINING LETTERS TO COMPLETE THE SENTENCE.

```
A  J  F  P  M  L  Q  W  N  B
I  Q  T  B  G  X  Y  G  T  H
M  H  V  Z  Y  D  Z  O  U  P
F  P  Z  ■  U  E  R  M  D  W
B  U  W  ■  B  V  J  F  X  O
R  S  Q  ■  N  P  A  V  Y  N
G  Y  Z  J  T  H  L  X  R  H
L  D  A  X  V  U  W  K  T  L
N  C  R  M  F  D  Q  G  J  A
```

IN THE VILLAGE OF HALLWIL, IN SWITZERLAND, A YOUNG GIRL DRESSES AS THE CHRISTMAS CHILD OR, "WIENECTCHIND," AND VISITS FAMILIES, GIVING CAKES AND __ __ __ __ __ __ __ TO CHILDREN.

UP OR DOWN?

UNSCRAMBLE THE WORDS, THEN IT'S UP TO YOU TO FIND WHERE EACH WORD GOES. WE PUT A FEW LETTERS IN TO HELP.

LAORCS _____

RSESD _____   I NBU _____

GILLAEV _____   BROE _____

ZADRWNETISL _____   ERSO _____

_____   LEBLS _____

RNTAELN _____   NLOE _____

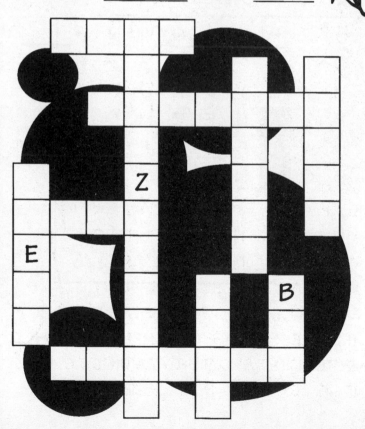

CAN YOU FIND THE WORDS?

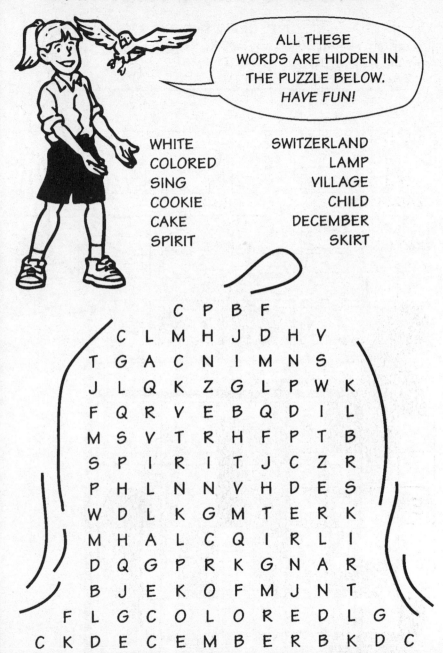

ALL THESE WORDS ARE HIDDEN IN THE PUZZLE BELOW. HAVE FUN!

WHITE
COLORED
SING
COOKIE
CAKE
SPIRIT

SWITZERLAND
LAMP
VILLAGE
CHILD
DECEMBER
SKIRT

```
        C P B F
      C L M H J D H V
    T G A C N I M N S
    J L Q K Z G L P W K
    F Q R V E B Q D I L
    M S V T R H F P T B
    S P I R I T J C Z R
    P H L N N V H D E S
    W D L K G M T E R K
    M H A L C Q I R L I
    D Q G P R K G N A R
    B J E K O F M J N T
  F L G C O L O R E D L G
C K D E C E M B E R B K D C
```

149

PICTURE MAKER

YOU MAKE THE PICTURE. DRAW THE IMAGE FROM EACH FRAME AT THE TOP IN THE FRAME BELOW WITH THE MATCHING NUMBER.

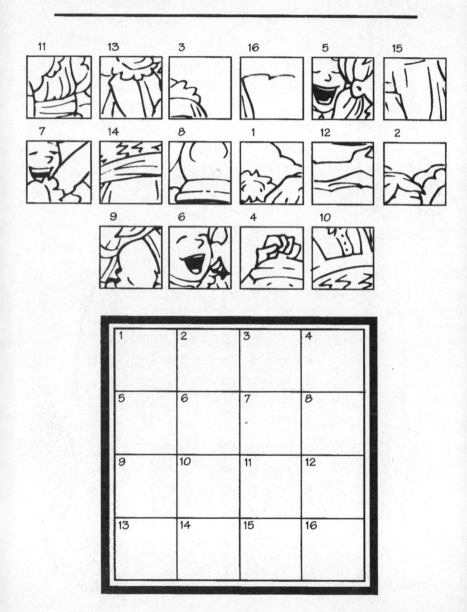

JUST A REGULAR OLD CROSSWORD!

ACROSS

1. GIVEN TO EACH OTHER
2. BOILED FOR DINNER
3. CHRISTMAS PLAY
4. WARM CAVITY IN HOME

DOWN

1. LIKE SPAIN AND NEXT DOOR
2. SALTED DRY FISH
3. BROUGHT IN FROM OUTSIDE
4. ALSO HOLDS PRESENTS

PICTURE MAKER

YOU MAKE THE PICTURE. DRAW THE IMAGE FROM EACH FRAME AT THE TOP IN THE FRAME BELOW WITH THE MATCHING NUMBER.

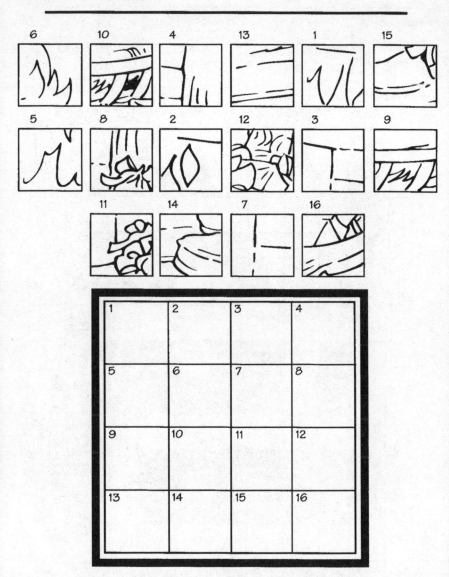

"BOAS FESTAS" IS PORTUGUESE FOR MERRY CHRISTMAS.

PICTURE CLUES

THE PICTURES ARE YOUR ONLY CLUES TO COMPLETING THIS CROSSWORD. THIS IS A BIT OF A BRAIN TEASER.

MERRY CHRISTMAS
FROM ALL OVER THE WORLD!

DON'T LEAVE IT SCRAMBLED!

UNSCRAMBLE EACH WORD, THEN USE THE CIRCLED LETTERS TO COMPLETE THE PUZZLE BELOW . . . AND I HOPE IT DOESN'T HURT YOUR EYES!

LLNFAYI, HET AYD ADH VRREDIA!

_ _ _ _ _ _ _ , _ _ _ _ _ _ _ _ _ _ _ _ _ _ !

HOCLSO SWA OELDSC FRO ETH

_ _ _ _ _ _ _ _ _ _ _ _ _ _ _ _ _

AIOLDSYH NAD LAL HTE SDKI

_ _ _ _ _ _ _ _ _ _ _ _ _ _ _ _

ERHSUD UTO, EAERG OFR HTAW

_ _ _ _ _ _ _ _ , _ _ _ _ _ _ _ _

AWS HDAEA. THMSASCRI ASW

_ _ _ _ _ _ _ . _ _ _ _ _ _ _ _ _ _ _

NOMGCI DAN HOW UWDLTON' EB

_ _ _ _ _ _ _ _ _ _ _ _ _ _ _ _

DECXTEI BTAUO ATTH?

_ _ _ _ _ _ _ _ _ _ _ _ ?

IT'LL BE

◯ ◯ ◯ ◯ ◯ ◯ ◯ ◯ ◯ SOON!

154

WHERE ARE THOSE VOWELS?

YOU'RE GOING TO HAVE TO CONCENTRATE FOR THIS ONE! VOWELS ARE HIDDEN IN THE PICTURE BELOW. YOU WILL NEED THEM TO COMPLETE THE PUZZLE.

SCH _ _ L'S _ _ T F _ R CHR _ ST-
M _ S, _ ND TH _ H _ L _ D _ YS
H _ V _ B _ G _ N!

TRAVELLIN' RHYMES

THIS IS A GREAT GAME TO PLAY AS YOU TRAVEL. YOU'LL NEED SOMEONE TO PLAY IT WITH, THOUGH, LIKE YOUR BROTHER OR SISTER OR FRIENDS.

BELOW IS A LIST OF WORD PAIRS THAT RHYME WITH EACH OTHER. YOUR JOB IS TO CALL OUT THE WORDS AND HAVE THE PLAYERS COME UP WITH THE SILLIEST RHYMES. WRITE THE BEST ON THE SPACES BELOW.

SNOW, GROW   PLAY, GRAY
BALL, HALL   SLED, FED
TREE, KNEE   GREEN, SCREEN
EAT, FEET   SKI, BEE

_____

_____

_____

_____

_____

_____

_____

It's a Mystery

THIS IS A GREAT GAME TO PLAY AS YOU TRAVEL. YOU'LL NEED SOMEONE TO PLAY IT WITH, THOUGH, LIKE YOUR BROTHER OR SISTER OR FRIENDS.

BELOW IS A LIST OF PHRASES THAT NEED TO BE COMPLETED. SHOW THIS PUZZLE TO EACH PLAYER, WHO PICKS A LETTER TO FILL IN THE BLANKS, AND THEN HAS TEN SECONDS TO GUESS THE PHRASE. MOVE ON TO EACH PLAYER UNTIL THE MYSTERY IS SOLVED! AS THE HOST OF THIS GAME, YOU GET TO CHECK OUT THE SOLUTION FROM THE ANSWER PAGES AT THE BACK (IF YOU NEED TO)!

_ I L _ N _   N _ _ H _ _,   _ O _ _

_ _ G _ _ .

_ _ _ _ _ S _ M _ S   _ R _ _ .

_ _ R _ _ _ _ A S   S _ _ C _ I _ _ S .

L _ _ _ _ E   _ _ _ N   _ _

_ _ _ H _ E _ _ _ .

_ E _ _ S   I _   _ _ R _ .

_ _ _   _ _ _ L _ E   D _ _ S   O _

C _ _ _ _ T _ A _ .

REALLY SILLY STORIES

YOU CAN PLAY THIS GAME BY YOURSELF, BUT IT'S A LOT MORE FUN TO PLAY WITH OTHERS.

ASK EACH PLAYER TO CALL OUT THE KIND OF WORD INDICATED IN EACH SPACE—A NOUN OR ADJECTIVE OR ADVERB, FOR EXAMPLE—AND PLACE THAT WORD IN THE APPROPRIATE SPACE. DO NOT TELL ANYONE WHAT THE STORY IS ABOUT— IT'S MORE FUN THAT WAY!

BELOW YOU'LL FIND A DESCRIPTION OF WHAT VERBS, NOUNS, ADJECTIVES, ADVERBS, ETC., ARE—JUST IN CASE YOU NEED A LITTLE HELP.

<u>VERB</u>: AN ACTION WORD, LIKE *WALK*, *RUN*, OR *FLY*. MAY BE *WALKED*, *RAN*, OR *FLEW*, IF <u>PAST TENSE</u> IS CALLED FOR.

<u>ADVERB</u>: MODIFIES A VERB AND USUALLY ENDS IN "LY." *SLOWLY* AND *CAREFULLY* ARE A COUPLE OF EXAMPLES.

<u>NOUN</u>: A PERSON, PLACE, OR THING, LIKE *BOY*, *BOAT*, OR *CAR*.

<u>ADJECTIVE</u>: DESCRIBES SOMEONE OR SOME-THING. *DIRTY*, *SILLY*, AND *BIG* ARE A FEW EXAMPLES.

<u>PLACE</u>: COULD BE A *COUNTRY* OR *CITY*, ETC.

<u>PLURAL</u>: MORE THAN ONE ITEM, SUCH AS *GIRLS* IS THE PLURAL OF *GIRL*.

NOW MOVE ON TO THE FOLLOWING PAGE TO PLAY THIS REALLY SILLY GAME!

REALLY SILLY STORIES

DON'T LOOK AT THE STORY BELOW. INSTEAD, FILL IN THE BLANKS IN THE LIST BELOW WITH THE REQUIRED WORDS. THEN FILL IN THE BLANKS IN THE STORY AND GET READY TO LAUGH UNCONTROLLABLY!

VERB—PAST TENSE _____

NOUN _____

NOUN _____

NOUN _____

NOUN _____

VERB _____

NOUN _____

NOUN _____

ADJECTIVE _____

NOUN _____

NOUN _____

TIME OF DAY _____

ADJECTIVE _____

NAME OF SEASON _____

NOUN _____

VERB—PAST TENSE _____

PLURAL NOUN _____

ADVERB _____

NOUN _____

NOUN _____

VERB—PAST TENSE _____

NOUN _____

VERB _____

WAYNE _____ ALL THE WAY _____ FROM SCHOOL. _____
    VERB (PAST TENSE)   NOUN   NOUN
WAS THE FIRST _____ OF THE _____ HOLIDAY AND HE
           NOUN   NOUN
COULD HARDLY _____ TO GET _____ AND PREPARE FOR THE
           VERB   NOUN
_____ THAT WAS _____. HE HEARD LAST _____ THAT IT
NOUN   ADJECTIVE   NOUN
WAS EVEN SUPPOSED TO _____ LATER IN THE
                          NOUN
_____! NOW, WASN'T THAT JUST _____? HE HAD
TIME OF DAY   ADJECTIVE
ALL HIS _____ GEAR TO GET OUT OF _____ AND
      NAME OF SEASON   NOUN
GET READY; HE _____ TO BE READY WHEN THE _____
        VERB (PAST TENSE)   PLURAL NOUN
WERE _____ WITH THAT WONDERFUL _____ STUFF. HE
    ADVERB   NOUN
NEEDED TO HAVE HIS _____ AND SKIS AND SNOW-
                  NOUN
BOARD _____ AND WAXED AND READY FOR _____.
   VERB (PAST TENSE)   NOUN
HOW WOULD HE EVER BE ABLE TO _____ TONIGHT?
                       VERB

CAN YOU FIND THE WORDS?

ALL THESE
WORDS ARE HIDDEN IN
THE PUZZLE BELOW.
HAVE FUN!

SHARE   MAGI
NATIVITY   ANGELS
BETHLEHEM   CHURCH
SHEPHERD   JOSEPH
GOD   GIVE
MARY   CHRISTMAS

```
        C A
        V N
    B J M Q G L Y S
  W E W O T E O B K N
  D J T N M G L Z D O M S
K S O H V A C S G V S T H R
E T S L B R T J L M F U A T
J M E E T Y U I U A L E R F
Z P P H P L C G V G V G E H
T S H E P H E R D I J P Z J
T G O M J R Z U G F T G B L
  C H R I S T M A S C Y M
  F W T B O V M W S G
  C H U R C H S P
```

PICTURE MAKER

YOU MAKE THE PICTURE. DRAW THE IMAGE FROM EACH FRAME AT THE TOP IN THE FRAME BELOW WITH THE MATCHING NUMBER.

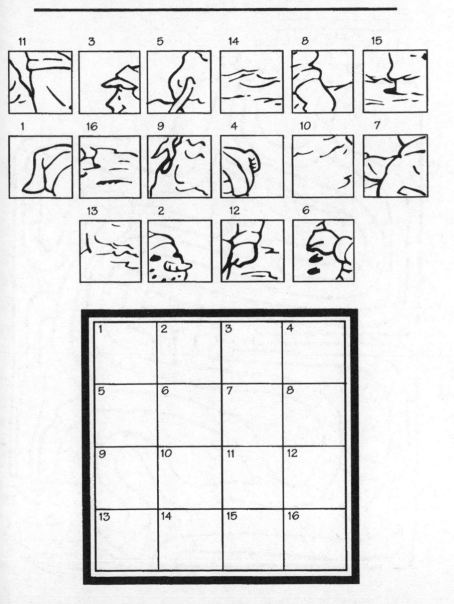

LET'S MAZE AROUND

SCHOOL'S OUT! HELP THE GANG GET HOME.

LESS SHALL BE FIRST

PLACE THE WORDS BELOW INTO THE PUZZLE ACCORDING TO THE NUMBER OF LETTERS IN EACH WORD, BEGINNING WITH THE WORD THAT HAS THE FEWEST LETTERS. THEN UNSCRAMBLE THE CIRCLED LETTERS TO COMPLETE THE ANSWER BELOW.

SNOWMAN INSTRUCTOR
SPOON PLAY
SHEPHERD SCHOOL
GOD CHRISTMAS

ENJOY THE

WHO, WHAT, WHERE

THIS IS A GREAT GAME TO PLAY AS YOU TRAVEL. YOU'LL NEED SOMEONE TO PLAY IT WITH, THOUGH, LIKE YOUR BROTHER OR SISTER OR FRIENDS.

BELOW IS A LIST OF QUESTIONS THAT NEED A "WHO, WHAT, OR WHERE" ANSWER. EACH PLAYER HAS TEN SECONDS TO ANSWER. AS THE HOST OF THIS GAME, YOU GET TO CHECK OUT THE SOLUTION FROM THE ANSWER PAGES AT THE BACK (IF YOU NEED TO)!

THIS MAN HAS A LOT TO TEACH YOU IF YOU SHOW UP ONCE A WEEK. *WHO* IS HE? _____

HE'LL SHOW YOU HOW TO GET DOWN THE MOUNTAIN SAFELY. *WHO* IS HE? _____

IT DOESN'T FLY, AND IT MAKES YOUR MOUTH WATER EVERY YEAR. *WHAT* IS IT? _____

IT IS VERY DIFFICULT WAITING TO FIND OUT THE CONTENTS OF THIS. *WHAT* IS IT? _____

AT THIS TIME OF YEAR, YOU'RE THINKING OF WHAT IS AHEAD . *WHERE* ARE YOU?

_____

164

FIND THE FOUR

COMPLETE THE PUZZLE BELOW BY CROSSING OUT EVERY LETTER THAT APPEARS AT LEAST FOUR TIMES. USE THE REMAINING LETTERS TO COMPLETE THE SENTENCE.

D	J	F	O	A	M	B	L	Q	U
C	I	X	P	S	Y	P	G	N	E
K	M	R	N	K	E	B	V	W	X
G	P	S	W	D	███		Q	C	J
N	L	Q	O	B	T	F	W	N	D
F	A	Y	I	G	C	S	I	M	V
O	C	X	K	Y	P	J	L	A	K
J	W	H	V	E	Y	X	O	V	Q
A	E	S	I	M	L	B	G	D	F

SNOWBALL FIGHTS ARE A LOT OF FUN, BUT TRY

NOT TO __ __ __ __ ANYONE!

TRAVELLIN' RHYMES

THIS IS A GREAT GAME TO PLAY AS YOU TRAVEL. YOU'LL NEED SOMEONE TO PLAY IT WITH, THOUGH, LIKE YOUR BROTHER OR SISTER OR FRIENDS.

BELOW IS A LIST OF WORD PAIRS THAT RHYME WITH EACH OTHER. YOUR JOB IS TO CALL OUT THE WORDS AND HAVE THE PLAYERS COME UP WITH THE SILLIEST RHYMES. WRITE THE BEST ON THE SPACES BELOW.

BOOK, HOOK   LIVE, GIVE

EGG, BEG   SLEIGH, TRAY

CANDY, HANDY   ICE, MICE

SCHOOL, COOL   PLAY, STAY

FLAKE, RAKE   BAND, HAND

_____

_____

_____

_____

_____

_____

_____

_____

JUST A REGULAR OLD CROSSWORD!

ACROSS

1. MUSIC PERFORMANCES
2. SNOW _____
3. FIRE BURNS IT
4. JUST LIKE SURFING
5. SEASONS MEANING
6. FISH THROUGH IT

DOWN

1. _____ HOLIDAY
2. SPECIAL SONGS
3. TEACHES ON MOUNTAIN
4. SKI _____
5. A SMALL TWIG
6. GOOD IN CABBAGE ROLLS

167

UP OR DOWN?

UNSCRAMBLE THE WORDS, THEN IT'S UP TO YOU TO FIND WHERE EACH WORD GOES. WE PUT A FEW LETTERS IN TO HELP.

ERTE _____

KURTYE _____

ENRTANSOM _____

NSRTEPE _____

HHBETELME _____

IANSGTK _____

A LITTLE FARTHER... AND YOU ARE *MINE!*

LETTER CLUES

TO DECODE THIS MESSAGE FROM GOD, YOU'LL NEED TO TAKE THE LETTER FROM EACH NUMBERED CLUE AND MATCH IT TO THE NUMBERED SPACE IN THE PUZZLE BELOW.

1. BEGINS THE WORD *NUT* AND ENDS THE WORD *MOON*.

   _____

2. APPEARS ONCE IN *ICE* AND TWICE IN *SKIING*.

   _____

3. THIS LETTER IS FOUND IN *BEGAN* BUT NOT IN *BEGUN*.

   _____

4. APPEARS TWICE IN *BOOT* BUT ONLY ONCE IN *POLE*.

   _____

5. FOUND TWICE IN BOTH *SNOWSHOE* AND *SOCKS*.

   _____

6. YOU'LL FIND THIS IN *LESS* BUT NOT IN *LOSS*.

   _____

7. BEGINS *TREE* AND IS IN THE MIDDLE OF *MOTOR*.

   _____

8. APPEARS ONCE IN *SISTER* AND TWICE IN *BROTHER*.

   _____

"Y_U W_LL B_ W__H CH_LD __D
  4   2   6   2 7   2   3 1

G_V_ B___H _____, ___D
 2 6   2 8 7   7 4 3 5 4 1   3 1

Y_U ____ __ G_V_ H_M _H_
 4   3 8 6 7 4   2 6   2   7 6

__M_ J___U_.'"
1 3 6 6 5 5

ALL JUMBLED UP

HEY . . . THIS ONE WILL BE FUN! FIND THE OPPOSITE OF EACH WORD, THEN USE THE CIRCLED LETTERS TO COMPLETE THE PUZZLE BELOW.

SNOW _ _ _ (_)

UP _ _ _ (_)

RECEIVE (_) _ _ _

DARK _ (_) _ _

FULL _ (_) _ _

HAPPY _ (_) _

SISTER _ _ _ _ _ (_) _

CHRIST, THE TRUE

(_) (_) (_) (_) (_) (_) (_)
_ _ _ _ _ _ _

OF CHRISTMAS.

170

DON'T LEAVE IT SCRAMBLED!

UNSCRAMBLE EACH WORD, THEN USE THE CIRCLED LETTERS TO COMPLETE THE PUZZLE BELOW... AND I HOPE IT DOESN'T HURT YOUR EYES!

ON NLBAOLWS GTIHF SI EOPMLETC

__ _____ ____ __ _____

HTUTOIW A NRFWOOTS OT RERTATE

_____ _ _____ __ _____

OT DAN EIHD NI. KMAE SA YANM

__ ___ ____ __. ____ __ ____

OSWN CRKISB SA DENEDE DAN

____ _____ __ _____ ___

TCAKS HMTE NO AHEC ORHET, KIGANM

_____ ____ __ ____ _____, _____

SREU HET ITNSOJ REA GGDTSREAE.

____ ___ _____ ___ _____.

U'YLOL EB BVNCEIINLI!

_____ __ _____!

YOU'LL NEED A

◯ ◯ ◯ ◯ ◯ ◯ ◯ ◯

171

REALLY SILLY STORIES

YOU *CAN* PLAY THIS GAME BY YOURSELF, BUT IT'S A LOT MORE FUN TO PLAY WITH OTHERS.

ASK EACH PLAYER TO CALL OUT THE KIND OF WORD INDICATED IN EACH SPACE—A NOUN OR ADJECTIVE OR ADVERB, FOR EXAMPLE—AND PLACE THAT WORD IN THE APPROPRIATE SPACE. DO NOT TELL ANYONE WHAT THE STORY IS ABOUT—IT'S MORE FUN THAT WAY!

BELOW YOU'LL FIND A DESCRIPTION OF WHAT VERBS, NOUNS, ADJECTIVES, ADVERBS, ETC., ARE—JUST IN CASE YOU NEED A LITTLE HELP.

<u>VERB:</u> AN ACTION WORD, LIKE *WALK, RUN,* OR *FLY.* MAY BE *WALKED, RAN,* OR *FLEW,* IF <u>PAST TENSE</u> IS CALLED FOR.

<u>ADVERB:</u> MODIFIES A VERB AND USUALLY ENDS IN "LY." *SLOWLY* AND *CAREFULLY* ARE A COUPLE OF EXAMPLES.

<u>NOUN:</u> A PERSON, PLACE, OR THING, LIKE *BOY, BOAT,* OR *CAR.*

<u>ADJECTIVE:</u> DESCRIBES SOMEONE OR SOMETHING. *DIRTY, SILLY,* AND *BIG* ARE A FEW EXAMPLES.

<u>PLACE:</u> COULD BE A *COUNTRY* OR *CITY,* ETC.

<u>PLURAL:</u> MORE THAN ONE ITEM, SUCH AS *GIRLS* IS THE PLURAL OF *GIRL.*

NOW MOVE ON TO THE FOLLOWING PAGE TO PLAY THIS REALLY SILLY GAME!

REALLY SILLY STORIES

DON'T LOOK AT THE STORY BELOW. INSTEAD, FILL IN THE BLANKS IN THE LIST BELOW WITH THE REQUIRED WORDS. THEN FILL IN THE BLANKS IN THE STORY AND GET READY TO LAUGH UNCONTROLLABLY!

VERB _____

NOUN _____

ADVERB _____

NOUN _____

ADJECTIVE _____

ADJECTIVE _____

NOUN _____

PLURAL NOUN _____

VERB—PAST TENSE _____

NOUN _____

ADJECTIVE _____

VERB _____

PLURAL NOUN _____

ADJECTIVE _____

NOUN _____

NOUN _____

NOUN _____

VERB (ENDING IN "ING")

NOUN _____

VERB (ENDING IN "ING")

_____

NOUN _____

ADJECTIVE _____

NOUN _____

FINALLY, THEY _____ AT THE TOP OF THE _____. THE DAY
      VERB   NOUN

_____ WAS FULL OF _____, WITH THE _____ OF
ADVERB   NOUN   ADJECTIVE

_____ RUNS DOWN FRESH _____. THEIR _____
ADJECTIVE   NOUN   PLURAL NOUN

WERE _____ AND POLISHED AND OFF SHE WENT. IT WAS AN
   VERB (PAST TENSE)

EXHILARATING _____ AS THEY TACKLED THE _____ RUN OF
            NOUN   ADJECTIVE

MANY THEY EXPECTED TO _____ THIS DAY. THEY KNEW
                         VERB

TO STAY OUT OF THE _____ MARKED _____ AND OFF-
               PLURAL NOUN   ADJECTIVE

LIMITS AND SO WOULD HAVE A _____ FILLED WITH _____ AND
                           NOUN   NOUN

_____. LATER, THEY LOOKED FORWARD TO _____ THEIR
NOUN   VERB—"ING"

TIME UP AT THE _____, _____ IN FRONT OF THE _____
             NOUN   VERB—"ING"   NOUN

AND WARMING THEMSELVES WITH _____ HOT _____.
                             ADJECTIVE   NOUN

TRAVELLIN' RHYMES

THIS IS A GREAT GAME TO PLAY AS YOU TRAVEL. YOU'LL NEED SOMEONE TO PLAY IT WITH, THOUGH, LIKE YOUR BROTHER OR SISTER OR FRIENDS.

BELOW IS A LIST OF WORD PAIRS THAT RHYME WITH EACH OTHER. YOUR JOB IS TO CALL OUT THE WORDS AND HAVE THE PLAYERS COME UP WITH THE SILLIEST RHYMES. WRITE THE BEST ON THE SPACES BELOW.

GLOVE, LOVE
BAKE, SNAKE
HORSE, COARSE
PLATE, GREAT

CAROL, BARREL
DINNER, THINNER
MEAT, FEET
SPELL, BELL

_____

_____

_____

_____

_____

_____

_____

_____

it's a MYSTERY

THIS IS A GREAT GAME TO PLAY AS YOU TRAVEL. YOU'LL NEED SOMEONE TO PLAY IT WITH, THOUGH, LIKE YOUR BROTHER OR SISTER OR FRIENDS.

BELOW IS A LIST OF PHRASES THAT NEED TO BE COMPLETED. SHOW THIS PUZZLE TO EACH PLAYER, WHO PICKS A LETTER TO FILL IN THE BLANKS, AND THEN HAS TEN SECONDS TO GUESS THE PHRASE. MOVE ON TO EACH PLAYER UNTIL THE MYSTERY IS SOLVED! AS THE HOST OF THIS GAME, YOU GET TO CHECK OUT THE SOLUTION FROM THE ANSWER PAGES AT THE BACK (IF YOU NEED TO)!

_ _ _   _ H _ _ E   _ _ _ _ E   M _ _ _.

T _ _ _ E _   W _ _ _   A _ _   T _ E
_ _ _ _ _ M _ _ _ G S.

_ _ R _ _ T,   _ _ _   S _ _ _ O _ _,
_ _   _ _ R _.

_ T _   B _ _ T _ R   _ _   _ _ _ _
_ _ A N   _ _   _ _ _ E _ V _ _.

C H _ _ _ _ T _ _ _   _ _ _ _.

_ _ _ _ R Y   _ _ _ _ _ S _ _ A S   A _ D
A   H _ _ _ _   _ _ _   _ _ A _!

175

CAN YOU PICTURE IT?

THE PICTURES ARE YOUR CLUES. USE THE CIRCLED LETTERS TO COMPLETE THE PUZZLE BELOW.

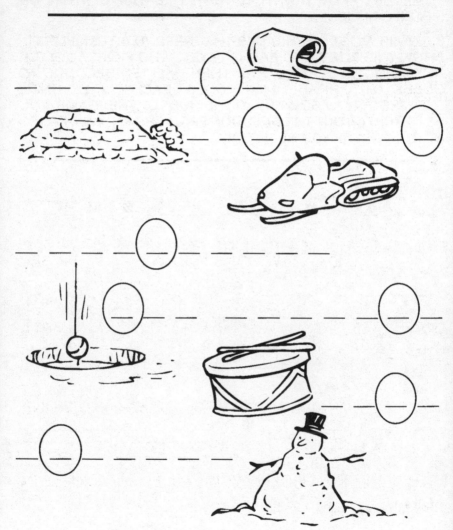

WHAT'S REALLY, REALLY BIG AND COVERED WITH SNOW?

WHO, WHAT, WHERE

THIS IS A GREAT GAME TO PLAY AS YOU TRAVEL. YOU'LL NEED SOMEONE TO PLAY IT WITH, THOUGH, LIKE YOUR BROTHER OR SISTER OR FRIENDS.

BELOW IS A LIST OF QUESTIONS THAT NEED A "WHO, WHAT, OR WHERE" ANSWER. EACH PLAYER HAS TEN SECONDS TO ANSWER. AS THE HOST OF THIS GAME, YOU GET TO CHECK OUT THE SOLUTION FROM THE ANSWER PAGES AT THE BACK (IF YOU NEED TO)!

SKIS HELP GET YOU QUICKLY FROM THE TOP TO THE BOTTOM. *WHERE* ARE YOU? _____

THIS PERSON RECEIVED A MIRACLE, AND THE SAVIOR WAS BORN. *WHO* WAS IT? _____

THREE MEN FROM THE EAST VISITED THIS SMALL TOWN. *WHERE* WERE THEY? _____

IT IS MADE WAY UP NORTH, BUT YOU CAN MAKE ONE TOO. *WHAT* IS IT? _____

WITH THIS AND A HORSE YOU CAN GO ANYWHERE IN THE SNOW. *WHAT* IS IT? _____

ON THIS, YOU ENJOY THE SAME SPORT IN WINTER AND SUMMER. *WHAT* ARE THEY? _____

PICTURE MAKER

YOU MAKE THE PICTURE. DRAW THE IMAGE FROM EACH FRAME AT THE TOP IN THE FRAME BELOW WITH THE MATCHING NUMBER.

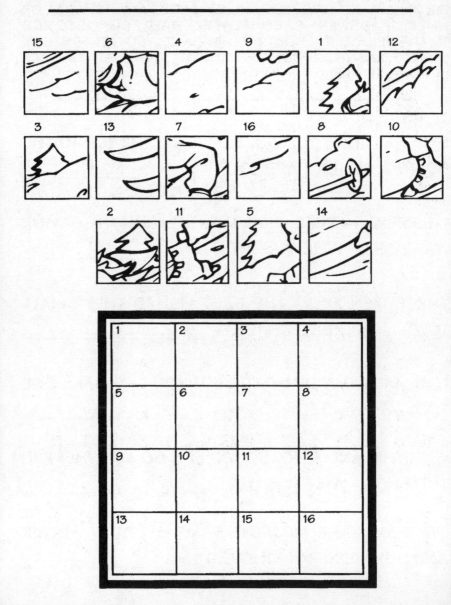

CAN YOU FIND THE WORDS?

ALL THESE WORDS ARE HIDDEN IN THE PUZZLE BELOW. *HAVE FUN!*

ORNAMENT
TREE
MANGER
SNOWBALL
GIFTS

JESUS
TURKEY
CANDY
ICE
SCHOOL

```
          Y E
        S W C Q T U
      B H N I F P H S Y R
        Z O J L C V D F
      P T W T M N N Z L B
    F G U B K R A D T R E E
      M R A J C Z N G Z M
    Q Y K L T B E F G K H T
  K S G E L Y M G J U E V T D
      U Y D A T R K E L R
    L C K N M Y N G P S W K
  Z V Y R L S C H O O L U Q F
  R N O F W Z C J G I F T S Y
          G S
```

FIND THE FOUR

COMPLETE THE PUZZLE BELOW BY CROSSING OUT EVERY LETTER THAT APPEARS AT LEAST FOUR TIMES. USE THE REMAINING LETTERS TO COMPLETE THE SENTENCE.

I	F	P	E	J	U	X	N	C	H
C	L	B	O	Q	V	T	W	L	W
A	H	K	G	M	P	I	U	D	Q
N	O	D	X	J	C	N	F	K	E
G	U	I	V	S	E	M	B	O	W
D	K	M	F	Y	V	G	Q	Y	■
J	W	P	Y	B	L	H	X	T	Y
L	B	N	X	G	M	P	I	U	K
H	V	Q	R	J	D	E	O	C	F

CHRISTMAS IS A TIME TO _ _ _ _ _

THINKING ABOUT OTHERS!

LESS SHALL BE FIRST

PLACE THE WORDS BELOW INTO THE PUZZLE ACCORDING TO THE NUMBER OF LETTERS IN EACH WORD, BEGINNING WITH THE WORD THAT HAS THE FEWEST LETTERS. THEN, UNSCRAMBLE THE CIRCLED LETTERS TO COMPLETE THE ANSWER BELOW.

DINNER
GIVE
HOLIDAYS
SKI

PRESENT
BETHLEHEM
IGLOO

TO YOU, A ⬡⬡⬡⬡⬡⬡ IS BORN.

REALLY SILLY STORIES

YOU CAN PLAY THIS GAME BY YOURSELF, BUT IT'S A LOT MORE FUN TO PLAY WITH OTHERS.

ASK EACH PLAYER TO CALL OUT THE KIND OF WORD INDICATED IN EACH SPACE—A NOUN OR ADJECTIVE OR ADVERB, FOR EXAMPLE—AND PLACE THAT WORD IN THE APPROPRIATE SPACE. DO NOT TELL ANYONE WHAT THE STORY IS ABOUT—IT'S MORE FUN THAT WAY!

BELOW YOU'LL FIND A DESCRIPTION OF WHAT VERBS, NOUNS, ADJECTIVES, ADVERBS, ETC., ARE—JUST IN CASE YOU NEED A LITTLE HELP.

<u>VERB:</u> AN ACTION WORD, LIKE *WALK, RUN,* OR *FLY.* MAY BE *WALKED, RAN,* OR *FLEW,* IF <u>PAST TENSE</u> IS CALLED FOR.

<u>ADVERB:</u> MODIFIES A VERB AND USUALLY ENDS IN "LY." *SLOWLY* AND *CAREFULLY* ARE A COUPLE OF EXAMPLES.

<u>NOUN:</u> A PERSON, PLACE, OR THING, LIKE *BOY, BOAT,* OR *CAR.*

<u>ADJECTIVE:</u> DESCRIBES SOMEONE OR SOMETHING. *DIRTY, SILLY,* AND *BIG* ARE A FEW EXAMPLES.

<u>PLACE:</u> COULD BE A *COUNTRY* OR *CITY,* ETC.

<u>PLURAL:</u> MORE THAN ONE ITEM, SUCH AS *GIRLS* IS THE PLURAL OF *GIRL.*

NOW MOVE ON TO THE FOLLOWING PAGE TO PLAY THIS REALLY SILLY GAME!

REALLY SILLY STORIES

DON'T LOOK AT THE STORY BELOW. INSTEAD, FILL IN THE BLANKS IN THE LIST BELOW WITH THE REQUIRED WORDS. THEN FILL IN THE BLANKS IN THE STORY AND GET READY TO LAUGH UNCONTROLLABLY!

NOUN _____

ADJECTIVE _____

PLURAL NOUN _____

VERB—PAST TENSE _____

VERB ENDING IN "ING"

_____

ADJECTIVE _____

VERB ENDING IN "ING"

_____

NOUN _____

PLURAL NOUN _____

NOUN _____

NOUN _____

NOUN _____

NOUN _____

PLURAL NOUN _____

NOUN _____

NOUN _____

PLURAL NOUN _____

NOUN _____

VERB _____

ADJECTIVE _____

PLURAL NOUN _____

ADJECTIVE _____

THE _____ WAS GETTING _____ AND HIGHER. KEVIN AND
   NOUN   ADJECTIVE

HIS THREE _____ HAD _____ THE MORNING _____ AN
         PLURAL NOUN VERB (PAST TENSE)   VERB—"ING"

_____ SNOW FORT AND WERE NOW _____ UP ON
 ADJECTIVE   VERB—"ING"

THE "AMMUNITION" THEY WOULD NEED. WITH THE _____
                                           NOUN

OF _____ THEY WERE AMASSING, THE OTHER _____
   PLURAL NOUN   NOUN

WOULD HAVE NO _____ AGAINST THEM IN THIS _____
            NOUN   NOUN

_____ THAT WAS SURE TO MAKE HISTORY! BOTH _____
 NOUN   PLURAL NOUN

HAD AGREED ON A _____ IT WOULD BEGIN, AND THAT LEFT
                NOUN

THEM AN _____ TO GO. AS THEY CONTINUED TO MAKE
         NOUN

_____ THEY DISCUSSED THEIR _____. THE OTHER GUYS
PLURAL NOUN   NOUN

WOULDN'T _____ A CHANCE! THEN, SUDDENLY A _____
        VERB   ADJECTIVE

OF _____ CAME AT THEM. IT WAS A _____ ATTACK!
  PLURAL NOUN   ADJECTIVE

PICTURE CLUES

THE PICTURES ARE YOUR ONLY CLUES TO COMPLETING THIS
CROSSWORD. THIS IS A BIT OF A BRAIN TEASER.

LET'S MAZE AROUND

THE CHURCH PLAY HAS ALMOST BEGUN. HELP THE GANG
FIND THEIR WAY IN THE DARK.

DON'T LEAVE IT SCRAMBLED!

UNSCRAMBLE EACH WORD, THEN USE THE CIRCLED LETTERS TO COMPLETE THE PUZZLE BELOW . . . AND I HOPE IT DOESN'T HURT YOUR EYES!

YVNREOEE   ELVOS   ICVEGERIN

_ _ _ _ _ _ _ _   _ _ _ _ _   _ _ _(_)_ _ _ _

FTIGS   TA   MRAHCTSSI   NDA   MEOS

_ _ _ _ _   _ _   _ _ _(_)_ _ _ _ _   _ _ _   _ _(_)_

VEHA   NVEE   ROSEEDVCDI   HET   OYJ

_ _ _(_)   _ _ _ _   _ _ _ _ _ _ _ _ _ _   _ _ _   _ _ _

AHTT   MESCO   NI   NIIGVG   SGFTI.

_ _ _ _   _ _(_)_ _ _   _ _   _ _ _ _ _ _   _ _ _ _ _.

IHTS   TUSMOC   SI   EASDB   NO

_ _ _ _   _ _ _ _ _ _   _ _   _ _(_)_ _   _ _

GTFIS   GOBRUTH   OT   HTE   OWBENRN

_ _ _ _ _   _ _ _ _ _ _ _   _ _   _ _(_)   _ _ _ _ _ _ _

EUSJS.

_ _ _ _ _.

OR MAGI, KINGS FROM THE EAST, CARRIED GIFTS FOR THE LORD.

186

TRAVELLIN' RHYMES

THIS IS A GREAT GAME TO PLAY AS YOU TRAVEL. YOU'LL NEED SOMEONE TO PLAY IT WITH, THOUGH, LIKE YOUR BROTHER OR SISTER OR FRIENDS.

BELOW IS A LIST OF WORD PAIRS THAT RHYME WITH EACH OTHER. YOUR JOB IS TO CALL OUT THE WORDS AND HAVE THE PLAYERS COME UP WITH THE SILLIEST RHYMES. WRITE THE BEST ON THE SPACES BELOW.

MERRY, DAIRY   RABBIT, HABIT
TOYS, BOYS   SLIDE, HIDE
CAT, MAT   PINE, DINE
DEER, STEER   SING, RING

_____

_____

_____

_____

_____

_____

LET'S MAZE AROUND

THE KIDS HAVE BEEN OUT PLAYING ALL DAY, AND THEY ARE FAMISHED! THEY'VE JUST BEEN CALLED FOR DINNER—HELP THEM FIND THE SHORTEST WAY HOME.

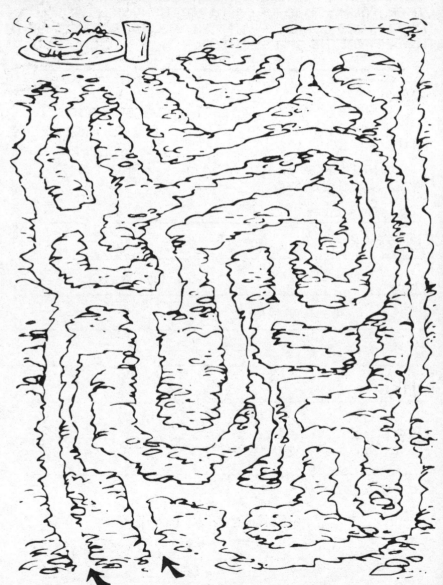

ALL JUMBLED UP

HEY ... THIS ONE WILL BE FUN! FIND THE OPPOSITE OF EACH WORD, THEN USE THE CIRCLED LETTERS TO COMPLETE THE PUZZLE BELOW.

SICK   _ _ _ _ _ ◯ _

RUN   ◯ _ _ _

BUY   ◯ _ _ _

UNWRAP   _ ◯ _ _

TEACH   _ _ _ _ ◯

FAST   _ _ ◯ _ _

SHRINK   _ ◯ _ _

LAST   ◯ _ _ _ _

A PLACE OF REFUGE:

◯ ◯ ◯ ◯   ◯ ◯ ◯ ◯
_ _ _ _   _ _ _ _

189

REALLY SILLY STORIES

YOU *CAN* PLAY THIS GAME BY YOURSELF, BUT IT'S A LOT MORE FUN TO PLAY WITH OTHERS.

ASK EACH PLAYER TO CALL OUT THE KIND OF WORD INDICATED IN EACH SPACE—A NOUN OR ADJECTIVE OR ADVERB, FOR EXAMPLE—AND PLACE THAT WORD IN THE APPROPRIATE SPACE. DO NOT TELL ANYONE WHAT THE STORY IS ABOUT— IT'S MORE FUN THAT WAY!

BELOW YOU'LL FIND A DESCRIPTION OF WHAT VERBS, NOUNS, ADJECTIVES, ADVERBS, ETC., ARE—JUST IN CASE YOU NEED A LITTLE HELP.

<u>VERB:</u> AN ACTION WORD, LIKE *WALK, RUN,* OR *FLY.* MAY BE *WALKED, RAN,* OR *FLEW,* IF <u>PAST TENSE</u> IS CALLED FOR.

<u>ADVERB:</u> MODIFIES A VERB AND USUALLY ENDS IN "LY." *SLOWLY* AND *CAREFULLY* ARE A COUPLE OF EXAMPLES.

<u>NOUN:</u> A PERSON, PLACE, OR THING, LIKE *BOY, BOAT,* OR *CAR.*

<u>ADJECTIVE:</u> DESCRIBES SOMEONE OR SOME-THING. *DIRTY, SILLY,* AND *BIG* ARE A FEW EXAMPLES.

<u>PLACE:</u> COULD BE A *COUNTRY* OR *CITY,* ETC.

<u>PLURAL:</u> MORE THAN ONE ITEM, SUCH AS *GIRLS* IS THE PLURAL OF *GIRL.*

NOW MOVE ON TO THE FOLLOWING PAGE TO PLAY THIS REALLY SILLY GAME!

REALLY SILLY STORIES

DON'T LOOK AT THE STORY BELOW. INSTEAD, FILL IN THE BLANKS IN THE LIST BELOW WITH THE REQUIRED WORDS. THEN FILL IN THE BLANKS IN THE STORY AND GET READY TO LAUGH UNCONTROLLABLY!

NAME _____

ADJECTIVE _____

NOUN _____

VERB (PAST TENSE) _____

VERB _____

NOUN _____

NOUN _____

NOUN _____

NOUN _____

ADJECTIVE _____

PLURAL NOUN _____

ADJECTIVE _____

NOUN _____

ADJECTIVE _____

NOUN _____

VERB (PAST TENSE) _____

NOUN _____

NOUN _____

VERB _____

ADJECTIVE _____

NOUN _____

JEFFEREY AND _____, ALONG WITH HER _____
           NAME   ADJECTIVE
_____, JIMMY HAD JUST _____ AT MAPLE TREE PARK
  NOUN   VERB (PAST TENSE)
AND WERE BEGINNING THE LONG _____ UP THE WESTWARD
                            VERB
_____. PULLING THE FRESHLY POLISHED _____ BEHIND
NOUN   NOUN
THEM, THEY HAD IN MIND TO SPEND THE _____ MAKING
                                      NOUN
_____ DOWN THIS _____ HILL. THERE WERE FEW
NOUN   ADJECTIVE
_____, AS IT WAS STILL _____ IN THE MORNING. AT
PLURAL NOUN   ADJECTIVE
LAST THEY ARRIVED AT THE _____ AND DECIDED TO MOVE
                          NOUN
OVER _____ _____ OR SO, AS ALONG THE WAY, THEY
     ADJECTIVE   NOUN
HAD _____ A RATHER NASTY LOOKING _____ UNDER
   VERB (PAST TENSE)   NOUN
THE _____ WHICH THEY WANTED TO _____.
       NOUN   VERB
FINALLY, THEY WERE OFF! WHAT A _____ _____
                               NOUN   ADJECTIVE   NOUN
THIS WAS GOING TO BE.

FIND THE FOUR

COMPLETE THE PUZZLE BELOW BY CROSSING OUT EVERY LETTER THAT APPEARS AT LEAST FOUR TIMES. USE THE REMAINING LETTERS TO COMPLETE THE SENTENCE.

```
B H Q I P C K R D S
S J N U D L N F I A
D W A S X Y U W T N
M P K G H B S M E K
Q ▮ F X C J P Y C X
C ▮ Q N Y T G H W Q
G U M X F W A R J B
R A T J U I P Y V R
M O I G H B T D F K
```

JESUS WAS BORN BECAUSE OF GOD'S LOVE FOR YOU! IN HIM, YOU TOO CAN __ __ __ __ OTHERS.

192

it's a MYSTERY

THIS IS A GREAT GAME TO PLAY AS YOU TRAVEL. YOU'LL NEED SOMEONE TO PLAY IT WITH, THOUGH, LIKE YOUR BROTHER OR SISTER OR FRIENDS.

BELOW IS A LIST OF PHRASES THAT NEED TO BE COMPLETED. SHOW THIS PUZZLE TO EACH PLAYER, WHO PICKS A LETTER TO FILL IN THE BLANKS, AND THEN HAS TEN SECONDS TO GUESS THE PHRASE. MOVE ON TO EACH PLAYER UNTIL THE MYSTERY IS SOLVED! AS THE HOST OF THIS GAME, YOU GET TO CHECK OUT THE SOLUTION FROM THE ANSWER PAGES AT THE BACK (IF YOU NEED TO)!

_ _ E _ _ _ _ T_ E D _ _ _ M _ _
_ O _ .

_ T _ _ _ _ _ _ _ _ _ _ H _ _ _ E _ .

P _ _ _ E _ _ _ _ _ _ T _ A _ _
_ _ _ D _ I _ _ _ _ _ _ _ N.

_ _ _ _ _ _ _ _ _ _ _ G I _ _
_ A _ _ _ R.

_ H _ _ E _ _ _ _ _ _ T _ A _ .

193

LETTER CLUES

TO DECODE THIS MESSAGE FROM GOD, YOU'LL NEED TO TAKE THE LETTER FROM EACH NUMBERED CLUE AND MATCH IT TO THE NUMBERED SPACE IN THE PUZZLE BELOW.

---

1. IT CAN BE FOUND IN *LAST* BUT NOT IN *LOST*.
   _____

2. LOOK FOR IT ONCE IN BOTH *TOY* AND IN *YELL*.
   _____

3. THIRD IN PLACE IN BOTH *RENT* AND IN *LENT*.
   _____

4. IT CAN BE FOUND IN *SONG* BUT NOT IN *SANG*.
   _____

5. IT DOUBLES BOTH *BOOTS* AND *TOBOGGANS*.
   _____

6. THIS LETTER BEGINS *ROUND* AND ENDS *HOUR*.
   _____

7. IT IS FOUND AT THE BEGINNING OF *JAM* AND *JOY*.
   _____

"W H E __   T H E __   __ __ W   T H E   __ T __ __,
     3   2   5 1   5   1 6

T H E __   W E __ E   __ V E __ __ __ __ E D.   __ __
     2   6   4   6 7 4 2   4 3

C __ M I __ G   T __   T H E   H __ U __ E,   T H E __
  4   3   4   4   5   2

__ __ W   T H E   C H I L D   W I T H   H I __   M __ T H E __
5 1   5   4   6

M __ __ __,   __ __ D   T H E __   B __ W E D   D __ W __
  1 6 2   1 3   2   4   4   3

__ __ D   W __ __ __ H I P E D   H I M."
1 3   4 6 5

MATTHEW 2:10–11

CAN YOU FIND THE WORDS?

ALL THESE WORDS ARE HIDDEN IN THE PUZZLE BELOW. *HAVE FUN!*

SILENT
HOLY
CANDLE
CONCERT
HOLIDAY

TOYS
MOUNTAIN
BELLS
TINSEL
HOLLY

```
                              W T Y
         R J K M Y K S Q H F H
       T R Z M T L T G W K O Z O
   B E L L S O D L I Z B L S L
   H W E Q H K U Y U N G L A I
   Q M S L U P F N H L S Y H D
   K G I B F K G L T T L E W A
   D Z L S Q T V J R A Q T L Y
   K T E D K H A E T W I R B J
   C A N D L E C P E V K N U W
   E B T Q F N K Z R F Q D G L
   L W U Y O G W M S L B N Q T
   M P F C E J L W F T P G Y P
   S G                 T O Y S
```

CAN YOU PICTURE IT?

THE PICTURES ARE YOUR CLUES. USE THE CIRCLED LETTERS TO
COMPLETE THE PUZZLE BELOW.

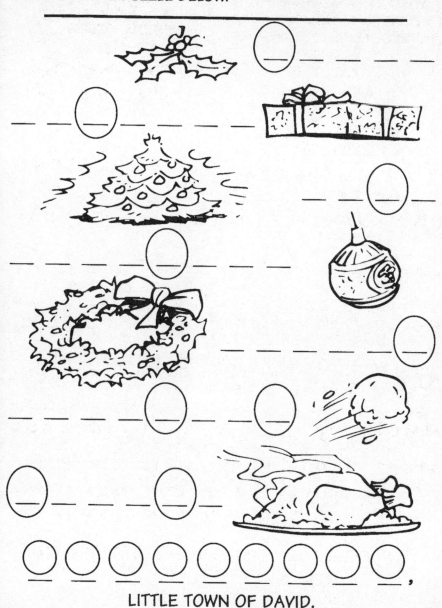

LITTLE TOWN OF DAVID.

196

DON'T LEAVE IT SCRAMBLED!

UNSCRAMBLE EACH WORD, THEN USE THE CIRCLED LETTERS TO COMPLETE THE PUZZLE BELOW ... AND I HOPE IT DOESN'T HURT YOUR EYES!

MIRHSTCAS   SI   OS   CMHU   FNU

_ _ _ _ _ _ _ _ _   _ _   _ _   _ _ _ _   _ _ _

NAD EYRVE ERYA VAEESL IGSTNAL

_ _ _   _ _ _ _ _   _ (_) _ _   _ _ _ _ _ _   _ _ _ _ _ _ _

ERSIMMOE.   PGEINKE NI DIMN OT

_ _ _ _ _ _ _ _ _.   _ _ _ _ _ _ _   _ _   _ _ _ _   _ _

EB   NCOTREAIEDS   OT   OTESH

_ _   _ _ (_) _ _ _ _ _ _ _   _ (_) _   _ _ (_) _ _

NRAODU OYU SALVEE UYO HWTI

(_) _ _ _ _ _   _ _ _   _ _ _ _ _   _ _ _   _ _ _ _

MMOEESIR   FO   A   RVYE   ICPEASL

_ _ _ _ (_) _ _ _   _ _   _   _ _ _ _   _ _ _ _ _ _ _

IDKN.

_ _ _ _.

A BLESSED CHRISTMAS IS IN BEING KIND TO

(_) (_) (_) (_) (_) (_).

197

PICTURE MAKER

YOU MAKE THE PICTURE. DRAW THE IMAGE FROM EACH FRAME AT THE TOP IN THE FRAME BELOW WITH THE MATCHING NUMBER.

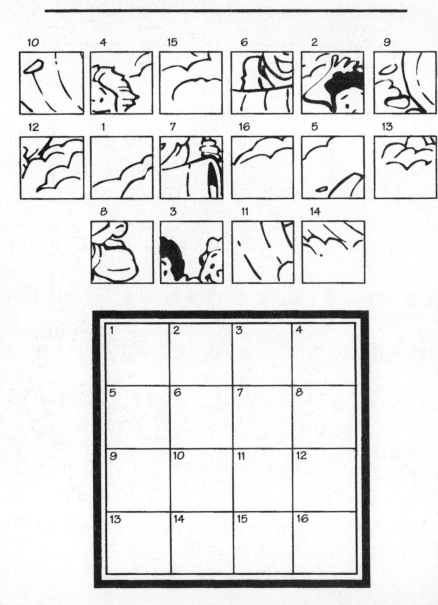

FIND THE FOUR

COMPLETE THE PUZZLE BELOW BY CROSSING OUT EVERY LETTER THAT APPEARS AT LEAST FOUR TIMES. USE THE REMAINING LETTERS TO COMPLETE THE SENTENCE.

```
N H I S T P K   V R D
A L Q B Z W X   U S N
P W Y M       J B Z L
D O J         A W Q
N X K         P A B
J D Z         F S V
C X L Y       D I Y E
V B S P G Y Z I N K
K Q I L W J Q V A X
```

THE WINTER SEASON IS FULL OF __ __ __ __ FUN
AND EXCITEMENT, BUT DON'T __ __ __ __ __ __
WHAT IT'S REALLY ABOUT.

REALLY SILLY STORIES

YOU *CAN* PLAY THIS GAME BY YOURSELF, BUT IT'S A LOT MORE FUN TO PLAY WITH OTHERS.

ASK EACH PLAYER TO CALL OUT THE KIND OF WORD INDICATED IN EACH SPACE—A NOUN OR ADJECTIVE OR ADVERB, FOR EXAMPLE—AND PLACE THAT WORD IN THE APPROPRIATE SPACE. DO NOT TELL ANYONE WHAT THE STORY IS ABOUT—IT'S MORE FUN THAT WAY!

BELOW YOU'LL FIND A DESCRIPTION OF WHAT VERBS, NOUNS, ADJECTIVES, ADVERBS, ETC., ARE—JUST IN CASE YOU NEED A LITTLE HELP.

<u>VERB:</u> AN ACTION WORD, LIKE *WALK*, *RUN*, OR *FLY*. MAY BE *WALKED*, *RAN*, OR *FLEW*, IF <u>PAST TENSE</u> IS CALLED FOR.

<u>ADVERB:</u> MODIFIES A VERB AND USUALLY ENDS IN "LY." *SLOWLY* AND *CAREFULLY* ARE A COUPLE OF EXAMPLES.

<u>NOUN:</u> A PERSON, PLACE, OR THING, LIKE *BOY*, *BOAT*, OR *CAR*.

<u>ADJECTIVE:</u> DESCRIBES SOMEONE OR SOMETHING. *DIRTY*, *SILLY*, AND *BIG* ARE A FEW EXAMPLES.

<u>PLACE:</u> COULD BE A *COUNTRY* OR *CITY*, ETC.

<u>PLURAL:</u> MORE THAN ONE ITEM, SUCH AS *GIRLS* IS THE PLURAL OF *GIRL*.

NOW MOVE ON TO THE FOLLOWING PAGE TO PLAY THIS REALLY SILLY GAME!

REALLY SILLY STORIES

DON'T LOOK AT THE STORY BELOW. INSTEAD, FILL IN THE BLANKS IN THE LIST BELOW WITH THE REQUIRED WORDS. THEN FILL IN THE BLANKS IN THE STORY AND GET READY TO LAUGH UNCONTROLLABLY!

NOUN _____

ADJECTIVE _____

NOUN _____

NOUN _____

VERB ENDING IN "ING" _____

_____

NOUN _____

NOUN _____

ADJECTIVE _____

NOUN _____

VERB (PAST TENSE)

_____

ADVERB _____

NOUN _____

NOUN _____

NOUN _____

PLURAL NOUN _____

PLURAL NOUN _____

ADJECTIVE _____

VERB _____

PLURAL NOUN _____

A _____ OF _____ SNOW COVERED THE _____
    NOUN   ADJECTIVE   NOUN

ON THIS CHRISTMAS _____. CHILDREN WERE _____
                  NOUN   VERB—"ING"

IN EVERY _____ AND EACH WAS FILLED WITH AWE AND
         NOUN

_____ AS THEY LOOKED _____. WHAT A BEAUTIFUL
 NOUN   ADJECTIVE

_____ THAT WOULD ACCOMPANY THEM AS THEY
 NOUN

_____ TO OPEN PRESENTS _____ THIS
VERB (PAST TENSE)   ADVERB

_____. WHAT A WONDERFUL _____ TO BE SO
 NOUN   NOUN

BLESSED WITH _____ AND PLENTY AND SECURITY. THEIR
           NOUN

_____ WOULD REMIND THEM THAT THERE WERE
PLURAL NOUN

SO MANY _____ NOT SO _____ AND THAT
      PLURAL NOUN   ADJECTIVE

THEY SHOULD BE SURE TO _____ THEM IN MIND AND IN
                  VERB

THEIR _____.
    PLURAL NOUN

JUST A REGULAR OLD CROSSWORD!

ACROSS

1. THINKING OF OTHERS
2. CHRISTMAS SCENE
3. TYPE OF TREE
4. CONSUMING FOOD
5. NICE TO WALK IN

DOWN

1. KIND TO OTHERS
2. TREE ORNAMENT
3. CHRISTMAS MEAT
4. TO STUMBLE
5. WIFE OF A CARPENTER

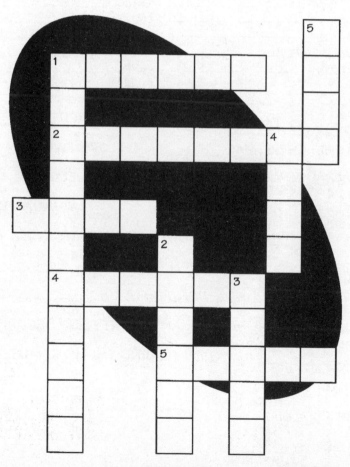

HERE ARE THE
ANSWERS!

Ⓙ U G G L E

R Ⓞ S E

D O N K Ⓔ Y

Ⓟ A R T Y Ⓗ A T

Ⓜ O U S E T R Ⓐ P

J Ⓔ R S Ⓔ Y

THEY WILL BE THE PARENTS OF JESUS. WHO ARE THEY?

Ⓙ Ⓞ S Ⓔ Ⓟ Ⓗ & Ⓜ Ⓐ R Ⓨ

6

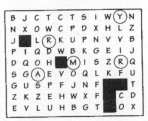

MARY AND JOSEPH PLAN TO M A R R Y.

7

"N I HET TXH SI OHNMT. DGO
IN THE SIXTH MONTH, GOD
TBNE ETH EALGN IAGBLER
SENT THE ANGEL GABRIEL
OT RZHTENAA. A ONWT NI
TO NAZARETH, A TOWN IN
EALLGIE. OT A NGIIVR
GALILEE, TO A VIRGIN
PDGELDE OT EB DMRAIRE
PLEDGED TO BE MARRIED
OT A ANM DMNEA HJSEPO.
TO A MAN NAMED JOSEPH,
A NCETPEASDN FO DVDIA."
A DESCENDANT OF DAVID."

LUKE 1:26-27

WHO IS THIS VISITOR?

Ⓖ Ⓐ Ⓑ Ⓡ Ⓘ Ⓔ L

8

"THE ANGEL WENT TO HER AND
SA ID, 'GREETINGS, YO U WHO ARE
HIGHLY FAVORED! THE LORD IS
WITH YO U."

LUKE 1:28

9

1. LOOK FOR THIS IN BOTH *RAFT* AND *HORSE*.
   ___

2. THIS ONE IS SEEN ONCE IN *RUG* AND TWICE IN *JUGGLE*.
   G

3. THIS LETTER IS FOUND TWICE IN *NONE* AND *NUN*.
   N

4. BEGINS THE WORD *HOT* AND ENDS THE WORD *TOUGH*.
   H

5. BEGINS THE WORD *OPEN* AND FOUND SECOND IN *ROPE*.
   O

6. THIS LETTER IS FOUND ONCE IN *YELLOW* AND *BABY*.
   Y

7. THIS LETTER CAN BE FOUND IN *WHEEL* AND *SWIM*.
   W

8. CAN BE SEEN THREE TIMES IN *TATTLE* AND ONCE IN *TOY*.
   T

9. *HOLY* HAS ONE BUT *HOLLY* HAS TWO.
   L

10. THIS LETTER IS FOUND IN *GIRLS* BUT NOT *GIRL*.
   S

"YOU WILL BE WITH C H I L D AND GIVE BIRTH TO
A SON, AND Y O U ARE T O GIVE HIM THE N A M E
J E S US.'"

LUKE 1:31

10

```
        M
      B A B Y
  S   A
  T   N
  A N G E L
  B   E
  L   R
S H E E P
  A       A
  N       I
  D       L
```

11

DBE	BED	LTEANBK	BLANKET
MLBA	LAMB	YOLHL	HOLLY
OEKYND	DONKEY	TSRA	STAR
CWO	COW	LBLE	BELL

```
            H
        B   C O W
        L   L
    B   A   L
  B E   N   L A M B
  E D O N K E Y     E
        E           L
        S T A R     L
```

12

MARY FINDS OUT THAT HER COUSIN, ELIZABETH,
WILL ALSO HAVE A C H I L D.

14

15

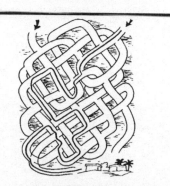

16

17

"WHEN ELIZABETH HEARD
MARY'S GREETING, THE BABY
LEAPED IN HER WOMB. AND
ELIZABETH WAS FILLED
WITH THE HOLY SPIRIT."

LUKE 1:41

20

"SCBEAEU SHEOJP RHE DSBHNUA

"BECAUSE JOSEPH HER HUSBAND

SWA A OGRIUHSTE ANM DAN

WAS A RIGHTEOUS MAN AND

IDD TNO TANW OT PSXOEE RHE

DID NOT WANT TO EXPOSE HER

OT UCLPIB AIGERDSC, EH DHA NI

TO PUBLIC DISGRACE HE HAD IN

DMNI OT RVOECDI EHR YUQLITE."

MIND TO DIVORCE HER QUIETLY"

MATTHEW 1:19

WHAT DID JOSEPH PLAN TO DO ABOUT THE WEDDING?

C A N C E L

21

THE LORD JESUS WAS BORN
IN BETHLEHEM.

THE MAGI BROUGHT GIFTS.

THERE WAS NO ROOM AT
THE INN.

A GREAT HOST OF ANGELS
APPEARED.

MARY, THE MOTHER OF THE
BABY JESUS.

A CHILD IS BORN, WHO
IS CHRIST, THE LORD.

22

M A S K

B L A N K E T

S W I N G

B I P L A N E

L A M P

S U N   H A T

WHO FOLLOWED THE STAR?

M A G I   FROM THE   E A S T

23

HSJEPO	JOSEPH	ATS	SAT
TTNE	TENT	NDE	DEN
RMREDIA	MARRIED	SJESU	JESUS
TEBALS	STABLE	SNO	SON

Crossword grid:

```
J O S E P H
  T
  M A R R I E D
  B       E
  L       N
  J E S U S
  E   A
  O   B
  N   T E N T
```

24

THIS YOUNG GIRL WAS VISITED BY AN ANGEL WITH
GOOD NEWS. *WHO* WAS SHE? _____ **MARY**
LUKE 1:26-33

THIS RULER WAS VERY AFRAID OF THE BIRTH OF
JESUS CHRIST. *WHO* WAS HE? _____ **HEROD**
MATTHEW 2:3

MARY TRAVELLED WITH JOSEPH TO THIS PROVINCE TO
GIVE BIRTH. *WHERE* WERE THEY? _____ **JUDEA**
LUKE 2:4

THIS PLACE WAS FULL, FORCING THE YOUNG COUPLE
TO GO ELSEWHERE. *WHAT* WAS IT? _____ **INN**
LUKE 2:7

HAVING BEEN WARNED, JOSEPH TOOK HIS FAMILY
HERE TO LIVE. *WHERE* ARE THEY? _____ **EGYPT**
MATTHEW 2:13-15

THIS LED MAGI FROM THE EAST TO THE BIRTHPLACE
OF CHRIST. *WHAT* WAS IT? _____ **STAR**
MATTHEW 2:9

25

Crossword grid:

```
    C H U R C H
    A       E
    E   S U I T
    S       A
    A       D
  C R O W N P H O N E S
            O
            N
        B I B L E
            L
            L
```

26

MOTHER	F A T H (E) R
SUN	(M) O O N
PEN	P (E) N C I (L)
DOG	C A (T)
DAY	N I G (H) T
COLD	(H) O T
STRAIGHT	(B) E N T
TIRED	A W A K (E)

WHERE DID THE MIRACLE BEGIN?
(B) (E) (T) (H) (L) (E) (H) (E) (M)

27

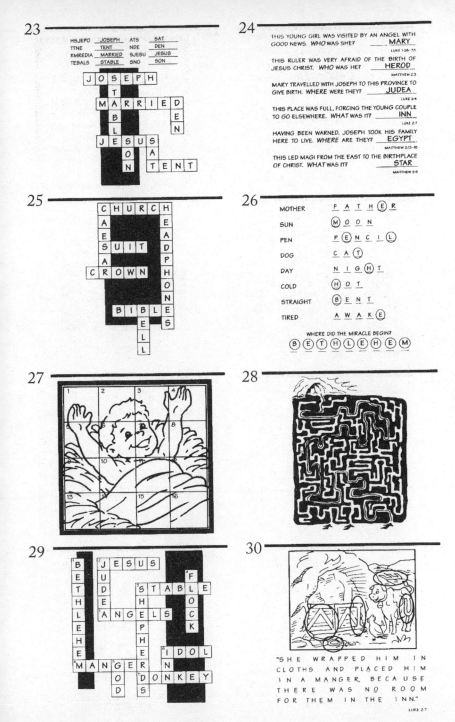

28

29

Crossword grid:

```
B   J E S U S
E   U           F
T   D   S T A B L E
H   E   H       O
L   A N G E L S C
E   E   P       C
H       H     I D O L
E       E
M A N G E R
        O D O N K E Y
        D
        S
```

30

"SHE WRAPPED HIM IN
CLOTHS AND PLACED HIM
IN A MANGER, BECAUSE
THERE WAS NO ROOM
FOR THEM IN THE INN."
LUKE 2:7

31

1. THIS LETTER BEGINS *HAIR* AND ENDS *ROUGH*.
   H
2. FOUND SECOND TO LAST IN BOTH *LOVE* AND *LEAVE*.
   V
3. FOUND ONCE IN *CRUMB* AND TWICE IN *ACCEPT*.
   C
4. THIS ONE'S TWICE IN *EFFECT* BUT ONCE IN *FAIR*.
   F
5. YOU'LL FIND THIS ONE IN *BEST* BUT NOT IN *BUST*.
   E
6. YOU'LL FIND THIS TWICE IN *BABY* AND ONCE IN *BOAT*.
   B
7. THIS LETTER BEGINS *GOAT* AND ENDS *JOG*.
   G

"AND THERE WERE SHEPHERDS LIVING OUT IN THE FIELDS NEARBY, KEEPING WATCH OVER THEIR FLOCKS AT NIGHT."

LUKE 2:8

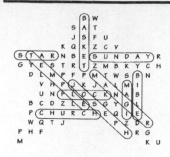

AN A N G E L APPEARS TO THE SHEPHERDS.

ISHHGTE	HIGHEST	WCAHT — WATCH
ONTW	TOWN	SHTO — HOST
GYLRO	GLORY	DLGA — GLAD
VLNYEEAH	HEAVENLY	ISH — HIS
DLRO	LORD	AEHRT — EARTH
HNEOS	SHONE	ERATH — HEART

35

SHEPHERDS WERE AT WORK, LOOKING AFTER THEIR SHEEP. *WHERE WERE THEY?* FIELDS
LUKE 2:8

SUDDENLY, SOMETHING SHONE ALL AROUND THEM. *WHAT WAS IT?* GLORY OF THE LORD
LUKE 2:9

HE BROUGHT THEM GOOD NEWS OF GREAT JOY FOR ALL PEOPLE. *WHO WAS HE?* ANGEL
LUKE 2:10

A SAVIOR HAD BEEN BORN WHO WAS CHRIST, THE LORD. *WHERE WAS HE BORN?* TOWN OF DAVID
LUKE 2:11

ALL GLORY WAS GIVEN TO HIM BY THE ANGELS AND ALL MEN. *WHO WAS HE?* GOD
LUKE 2:14

HE HAD NO BED, BUT THEY FOUND A PLACE TO LAY HIM DOWN. *WHAT WAS IT?* MANGER
LUKE 2:12

PEACE WAS GIVEN TO THEM ON WHOM RESTED THE FAVOR OF GOD. *WHO WERE THEY?* MEN
LUKE 2:14

36

"LDSUYNDE A RTEAG MCAYNOP FO
—SUDDENLY A GREAT COMPANY OF
HET VHNEEAYL STHO EEAARPDP WHTI
THE HEAVENLY HOST APPEARED WITH
ETH NEALG, IISPRGAN DGO NDA
THE ANGEL, PRAISING GOD AND
NASYGI, 'OGLRY OT ODG NI HET
SAYING, 'GLORY TO GOD IN THE
EIHSTGH, NAD NO TERAH ECPEA
HIGHEST, AND ON EARTH PEACE
OT NME NO OWMH ISH AFRVO
TO MEN ON WHOM HIS FAVOR
TRSES.'"
RESTS.'"

LUKE 2:13-14

THE HOST OF ANGELS
P R A I S E D GOD.

42

H	E	A	M	B	S	G	P	H	C
C	K	P	J	G	N	F	(L)	T	J
I	H	(R)	Q	T	K	U	E	S	N
P	Q	V	K	I	U	B	Y	G	H
F	B	T	W	F	M	Q	V	W	X
J			Y	X	P	S	Y	A	T
M	X	A	E	Q	(O)	J	I	N	C
V	Y	X	G	U	W	K	C	U	F
A	W	V	I	M	(D)	B	E	N	S

JESUS IS OUR SAVIOR AND OUR L O R D.

43

DIRSHPW	WORSHIP
RADME	DREAM
RHEYM	MYRRH
RTMHFO	MOTHER
TOYRNCU	COUNTRY
PFRHOTE	PROPHET

45

46

A N G E L

G I F T

P I G

S T A F F

M O O N

E G Y P T

WHAT DID THE ANGEL TELL JOSEPH IN HIS DREAM?
G O   T O   E G Y P T

47

48

49

AN ANGEL TOLD THIS MAN, IN A DREAM, TO ESCAPE TO EGYPT. *WHO* WAS HE?   **JOSEPH**
MATTHEW 2:13

THE FAMILY OF JESUS STAYED HERE UNTIL THE DEATH OF HEROD. *WHERE* WERE THEY?   **EGYPT**
MATTHEW 2:14-15

THEY MIGHT HAVE SEEN SOMETHING INCREDIBLE ON ARRIVAL. *WHAT* WAS IT?   **THE PYRAMIDS**

50

M	B	L	F	T	J	W	M	V	(O)
I	(E)	V	C	S	A	P	U	G	Q
K	T	W	N	Q	X	Y	N	X	J
L	G	J	Z	I	Z	L		A	Y
C	S	X	B	Z	F	Q	Z	C	B
P	N	(R)	Y	K	T	N	P	U	G
A	V	M	Q	F	S	G	Y	X	W
U	F	W	L	C	J	B	V	(H)	M
K	I	(D)	T	P	U	A	I	K	S

AFTER THE DEATH OF H E R O D , THE FAMILY OF JESUS RETURNED TO NAZARETH.

HERE ARE THE
ANSWERS!

51

54

THEY TRAVELLED A GREAT DISTANCE TO SEE A NEW-BORN KING. *WHO* WERE THEY?   MAGI

IT IS A MESSAGE OF JOY AND COMES ONCE EVERY YEAR. *WHAT IS IT?*   CHRISTMAS

IF THIS KING HAD GOTTEN HIS WAY, THERE WOULD BE NO CHRISTMAS. *WHO* WAS HE?   HEROD

A MIRACULOUS STAR SHONE BRIGHTLY OVER THIS LITTLE TOWN. *WHERE* WAS IT?   BETHLEHEM

IT'S ONE WAY WE RE-LIVE THE SPIRIT OF CHRISTMAS WITH LOVED ONES. *WHAT IS IT?*   GIFTS

55

GNLEA — ANGEL
MRSISTHAC — CHRISTMAS
YMFALI — FAMILY
VROSAI — SAVIOR
NMGIDKO — KINGDOM
LKACB — BLACK
MIGA — MAGI
EUDAJ — JUDEA
TGSFI — GIFTS
LDGA — GLAD

58

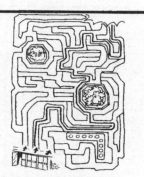

60

CARVING
COOKING
SKIING
TOBOGGAN
PHONE
TRIM

CHRISTMAS IS ABOUT
GIVING,
NOT GETTING.

61

62

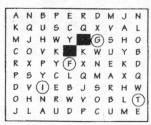

JESUS IS OUR G I F T FROM GOD.

63

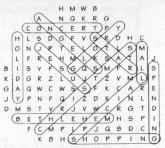

A word search puzzle with letters. Circled words include: CONCERT, BETHLEHEM, SHOPPING, HOLIDAY, GIFTS, and others.

64

Crossword with: HEART, KIND, MIRACLE, FRIENDS, LOVE, DECORATE, SNOWSHOES, GLOW

65

Grid numbered 1–16.

66

"AFTER JESUS WAS BORN IN BETHLEHEM IN JUDEA, DURING THE TIME OF KING HEROD, MAGI FROM THE EAST CAME TO JERUSALEM AND ASKED, 'WHERE IS THE ONE WHO HAS BEEN BORN KING OF THE JEWS? WE SAW HIS STAR IN THE EAST AND HAVE COME TO WORSHIP HIM.'"

MATTHEW 2:1-2

67

HOT
BAND
GLORY
MOTHER
FRIENDS
PRESENTS
TRIMMINGS
TELEVISION

TO GIVE IS BETTER THAN TO RECEIVE!

70

1. THIS LETTER IS FOUND BOTH IN *BIN* AND IN *FIN*. I
2. THIS LETTER BEGINS BOTH THE WORDS *DESK* AND *DOG*. D
3. THIS LETTER IS FOUND IN *TALK* BUT NOT IN *WALK*. T
4. THIS LETTER IS FOUND IN *MAZE* BUT NOT IN *HAZE*. M
5. IT APPEARS TWICE IN *BABY* AND ONCE IN *BELL*. B
6. THIS LETTER IS FOUND IN *WING* BUT NOT IN *SING*. W
7. THE SAME LETTER IS FOUND ONCE IN *COARSE* AND IN *SIT*. S

"THIS IS HOW THE BIRTH OF JESUS CHRIST CAME ABOUT: HIS MOTHER MARY WAS PLEDGED TO BE MARRIED TO JOSEPH, BUT BEFORE THEY CAME TOGETHER, SHE WAS FOUND TO BE WITH CHILD THROUGH THE HOLY SPIRIT."

MATTHEW 1:18

71

HE ASKED THE MAGI TO RETURN TO HIM, AS HE HAD EVIL IN MIND. *WHO* WAS HE? **KING HEROD**

HE GREW FROM HUMBLE BEGINNINGS TO BE THE SAVIOR OF ALL. *WHO* WAS HE? **JESUS**

JESUS' FAMILY RETURNED TO LIVE HERE AFTER EXILE IN EGYPT. *WHERE* WERE THEY? **NAZARETH**

IT LED THESE MEN OVER A LONG DISTANCE TO SEE A MIRACLE. *WHAT* WAS IT? **STAR OF BETHLEHEM**

THROUGH HIS POWER, MARY CONCEIVED A BLESSED CHILD. *WHO* WAS HE? **HOLY SPIRIT**

THE MAGI BROUGHT SOMETHING SPECIAL TO JESUS. *WHAT* WAS IT? **INCENSE, GOLD, MYRRH**

72

THE BEST PRESENT WE HAVE EVER RECEIVED IS JESUS. HE IS GOD'S GREATEST GIFT TO US, GIVEN IN LOVE TO ALL PEOPLE.

73

THE BEST PRESENT EVER.

THE KING OF THE JEWS.

NAZARETH, A TOWN IN GALILEE.

GLORY TO GOD IN THE HIGHEST.

THE ANGEL OF THE LORD.

74

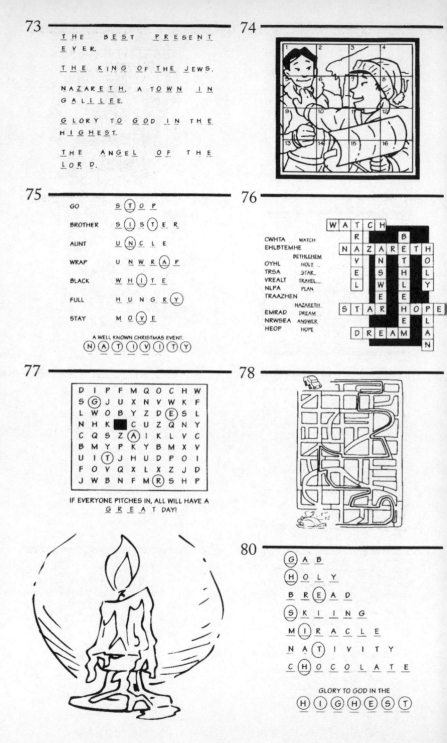

75

GO	S T O P	
BROTHER	S I S T E R	
AUNT	U N C L E	
WRAP	U N W R A P	
BLACK	W H I T E	
FULL	H U N G R Y	
STAY	M O V E	

A WELL KNOWN CHRISTMAS EVENT.
N A T I V I T Y

76

CWHTA — WATCH
EHLBTEMHE — BETHLEHEM
OYHL — HOLY
TRSA — STAR
VREALT — TRAVEL
NLPA — PLAN
TRAAZHEN — NAZARETH
EMRAD — DREAM
NRWSEA — ANSWER
HEOP — HOPE

W A T C H
NAZARETH
STAR HOPE
DREAM

77

D I P F M Q O C H W
S G J U X N V W K F
L W O B Y Z D E S L
N H K ■ C U Z Q N Y
C Q S Z A I K L V C
B M Y P K Y B M X V
U I T J H U D P O I
F O V Q X L X Z J D
J W B N F M R S H P

IF EVERYONE PITCHES IN, ALL WILL HAVE A
G R E A T DAY!

78

80

G A B
H O L Y
B R E A D
S K I I N G
M I R A C L E
N A T I V I T Y
C H O C O L A T E

GLORY TO GOD IN THE
H I G H E S T

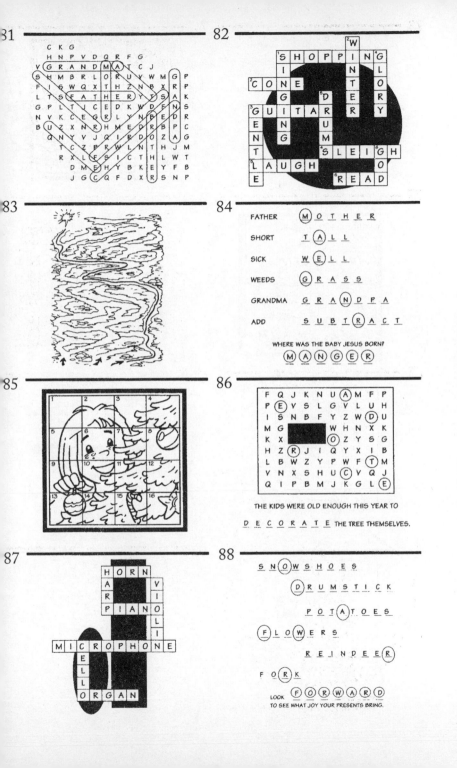

81

82

83

84

FATHER — M O T H E R

SHORT — T A L L

SICK — W E L L

WEEDS — G R A S S

GRANDMA — G R A N D P A

ADD — S U B T R A C T

WHERE WAS THE BABY JESUS BORN?
M A N G E R

85

86

THE KIDS WERE OLD ENOUGH THIS YEAR TO

D E C O R A T E THE TREE THEMSELVES.

87

HORN
HARP · VIOLIN
PIANO
MICROPHONE
CELLO
ORGAN

88

S N O W S H O E S

D R U M S T I C K

P O T A T O E S

F L O W E R S

R E I N D E E R

F O R K

LOOK F O R W A R D
TO SEE WHAT JOY YOUR PRESENTS BRING.

89

"RLYOG OT DGO NI HET SGEHITH, NAD
"GLORY TO GOD IN THE (H)IGHEST, AND
NO ATREH CEEPA OT ENM NO OWMH
ON EARTH PEA(C)E(T)O MEN ON WHOM
ISH VOAFR TRSES."
H(I)S FAVOR (R)ES(T)S."

LUKE 2:14

THE GREATEST GIFT?
(C) H (R) I (S) T

90

91

SA OGD EGVA OYU IHS ETSB
AS GOD GAVE YOU HIS B(E)ST
NEKESPT, UYO OTO LOUHDS IGEV
(P)RESENT, YOU TOO SHOULD GIVE
OT HRTEOS ROYU OELV DAN
TO OTHERS YOU(R) LOVE AND
NNDISESK. OT IVEG TISH OT
KIND(N)ESS. TO GIVE TIS OT
HNTOERA SI RAF OREM BAAULLVE
HNTOERA SI RAF OREM BAAULLVE
ANOTHER IS FAR MORE VALUABLE
TANH YGNHITNA ELSE.
THAN ANY(T)HING EL(S)E.

GIVE YOUR BEST
(P) (R) (E) (S) (E) (N) (T)

94

"BUT THE ANGEL SAID TO THEM,
'DO NOT BE AFRAID. I BRING
YOU GOOD NEWS OF GREAT JOY
THAT WILL BE FOR ALL THE PEOPLE.
TODAY IN THE TOWN OF DAVID A
SAVIOR HAS BEEN BORN TO YOU; HE
IS CHRIST THE LORD.'"

LUKE 2:10-11

95

```
        G R A N D M A
                    A
      S T U F F I N G
      O             I
      G O B L E T
      G
B     G       T
E   M A N G E R   B
L   N         A   A
L             V   N
S H O R T B R E A D
              L
```

96

```
C N R (L) K E P H C F
G I O V D U Q B S J
T P H W J F N T M G
(A) D T E S R O ■ U W
S ■ K U B G ■ E V C
J R W C O V D P I N
O M F V I W R U (L) Q
E Q T H P K Q M S H
K B I M D G N B F J
```

MOM'S GOT A BUSY DAY AHEAD, AND RATHER THAN
PLAY WITH THEIR NEW TOYS A L L DAY, THE
KIDS ARE HELPING TO PREPARE CHRISTMAS DINNER.

97

ONLY TWO DA Y S OF
SHOPP I NG LEFT!

DECORAT I NG THE
CHRISTMAS TREE.

SNOWBALL F I GHT.

TURKEY WITH ALL
THE TRIMMINGS.

DECK THE HALLS
WITH BOUGHS OF
HOLL Y.

HERE ARE THE
ANSWERS!

99

NI GBLEUMI, MRSITSAHC SI
IN BELGIUM, CHRISTMAS IS
BTELDAECRE NO TMHRSSIAC VEE.
CELEBRATED ON CHRISTMAS EVE.
IHTW A ELMA FO FOSAEDO NAD
WITH A MEAL OF SEAFOOD AND
YRTKUE. A NARTADLOTI RSDESTE
TURKEY. A TRADITIONAL DESSERT
SI A ECKA MDEA IHWT MCEAR,
IS A CAKE MADE WITH CREAM,
LDLEAC A CRSMATISH GLO.
CALLED A CHRISTMAS LOG.
SNSPRETE REA NEPDEO YAREL.
PRESENTS ARE OPENED EARLY
NO CRBDMEEE TXSIHI
ON DECEMBER SIXTH.

A SPECIAL SWEET BREAD FOR BREAKFAST IS CALLED

C O U G N O U

100

101

LCOSHANI	NICHOLAS	UCEL	CLUE
EUMIGLB	BELGIUM	ESSTRDE	DESSERT
PRFIEECLA	FIREPLACE	RWCNO	CROWN
GCKNITSOS	STOCKINGS	ETFAHR	FATHER
MEDEER	REDEEM	EGTA	GATE

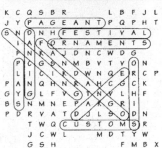

"ZALIG KERSTFEET" MEANS MERRY CHRISTMAS IN BELGIUM!

102

IN BRAZIL, THEY ENJOY F O L K PLAYS
AT CHRISTMAS.

103

104

105

MERRY S A D

DINNER B R E A K F A S T

SOUTH N O R T H

RECORDED L I V E

STRAIGHT Z I G - Z A G

SLEEP A W A K E

RUN W A L K

IN BRAZIL, "BOAS FESTAS E FELIZ
ANO NOVO," MEANS HAPPY HOLIDAYS.

B O X I N G D A Y I S T H E B I G
C H R I S T M A S C E L E B R A T I O N
I N E N G L A N D A N D I S A
N A T I O N A L H O L I D A Y . B O X E D
P R E S E N T S , P L A C E D I N C H U R C H E S
T H R O U G H O U T T H E Y E A R , A R E
O P E N E D O N T H I S D A Y .

L E D
A C T S
B O X E D
S T O N E D
H O L I D A Y
N A T I O N A L
P R I N C I P L E

THIS DAY IS ALSO CALLED
SAINT S T E P H E N DAY,
AFTER THE CHRISTIAN MARTYR WHO WAS STONED
TO DEATH, AS TOLD IN THE BOOK OF ACTS.

E	N	I	D	J	S	B	F	G	A
M	K	Q	U	G	P	W	V	M	Q
C	F	W	X	A	Q	D	S		I
O	J	X	L	U	M	J	H		B
G	V	B	H	N	T	K	W	L	X
S	P	U	C	O	I	G	A	O	V
A	N	D	J	Q	F	W	P	V	D
H	K	M	X	R	S	C	L	U	F
L	C	P	H	O	B	K	N	I	E

LEGEND TELLS US THAT IT WAS IN GERMANY WHERE
THE CHRISTMAS T R E E WAS SUPPOSEDLY
FIRST INTRODUCED.

THEY FIRST BEGAN TO BRING THESE INTO THEIR
HOMES. *WHAT* IS IT? _____ CHRISTMAS TREE

HE WAS THE ONE BEHIND THE REFORMATION AND A
CHRISTMAS SYMBOL. *WHO* IS HE? MARTIN LUTHER

A HUGE TOY FAIR KICKS OFF CHRISTMAS IN THIS
COUNTRY. *WHERE* IS IT? _____ GERMANY

GERMANS LOVE TO DECORATE AROUND A FRAME THAT
CAN BE SEEN OUTSIDE. *WHAT* IS IT? _____ WINDOW

GERMANS LOVE TO HEAR THIS GROUP WHO VISIT
THEIR HOMES. *WHO* ARE THEY? _____ CAROLERS

112

O T A N N E N B A U M.

T H E A D V E N T C A L E N D A R
I S A T R A D I T I O N I N
G E R M A N Y.

I N G E R M A N Y, P O P U L A R
T R E A T S A R E F I G U R E S M A D E
O F S U G A R Y M A R Z I P A N
D O U G H.

T O S A Y M E R R Y C H R I S T M A S
I N G E R M A N W O U L D B E,
"F R O E C H L I C H E W E I N N A C H T E N."

F O R C H I L D R E N, A T O Y
F A I R I S T H E B E S T W A Y
T O B E G I N C H R I S T M A S.

	¹P	A	R	T	Y				
	A				³C				
²C	H	R	I	S	T	M	A	S	
	A			W	N			⁵D	
⁴R	E	D		E	D			A	
	O			D	E		⁶P	L	A	Y
	B			E	N			E	
	E			N			⁷S	U	N

IN THIS COUNTRY, THE SHORTEST, DARKEST DAY IS
DECEMBER 22. *WHERE* IS IT? _____ SWEDEN

A SPECIAL MEAL IS EATEN ON THIS MOST IMPOR-
TANT DAY. *WHAT* DAY IS IT? CHRISTMAS EVE

IN SWEDEN, MANY GO HERE TO MEET ON CHRIST-
MAS MORNING. *WHERE* IS IT? _____ CHURCH

BECAUSE OF WINTER DARKNESS, THESE ARE VERY
IMPORTANT. *WHAT* ARE THEY? _____ CANDLES

KRINGLE, KRUMKAKE, AND SANDBAKKELS ARE
TRADITIONAL. *WHAT* ARE THEY? _____ SWEETS

AN IMPORTANT FIGURE IN SWEDISH TRADITION WHO
WAS MARTYRED. *WHO* IS SHE? _____ ST. LUCIA

115

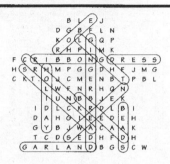

116

BELIEF	D O U B T
NIGHT	D A Y
BLACK	W H I T E
YOUNG	O L D
FORWARD	B A C K W A R D
SIT	S T A N D
CROOKED	S T R A I G H T

LONG AGO, A YOUNG SWEDISH GIRL WAS KILLED FOR HER CHRISTIAN BELIEFS AND IS NOW KNOWN AS S T. L U C I A SHE IS REMEMBERED ON DECEMBER 13, WHICH IS NOW A SPECIAL DAY IN THE SWEDISH CHRISTMAS.

117

```
          B L E J
        D G B E L N
      K O L G Q P
      R H P I M K
F C R I B B O N G D R E S S
H S R H M P G G D H E J M G
C K T O U C M E N B T P B L
      L W F N R H O N
      I D L C K R D L B I
      D A H G X E E D E H
      G Y B J W A C A A K
      T C D S E D H F D H
G A R L A N D B G S C W
```

118

1. THIS LETTER IS FOUND IN BOTH *DRESS* AND *GET*.
   E
2. IT'S FOUND ONCE IN *ROBE* AND TWICE IN *RIBBON*.
   B
3. FOUND FIRST IN BOTH *CANDLES* AND IN *CANDY*.
   C
4. FOUND FIRST IN BOTH *FRANCE* AND IN *FRENCH*.
   F
5. THIS LETTER BEGINS *X-RAY* AND ENDS *BOX*.
   X
6. THIS LETTER IS FOUND IN *REST* BUT NOT IN *BEST*.
   R

IN FRANCE, CHRISTMAS TREES ARE DECORATED WITH WHITE CANDLES AND RED RIBBONS. EVEN TREES OUTSIDE ARE DECORATED AND LIT THROUGH THE NIGHT. IN THE LANGUAGE OF THE FRENCH, ONE WOULD HEAR MERRY CHRISTMAS AS, "JOYEUX NOEL"

119

B O W
R O B E
B R E A D
W I N D O W
H O L I D A Y
P I C T U R E S
B E A U T I F U L

CANDLES AND R I B B O N S ARE A PART OF A FRENCH CHRISTMAS.

120

OESTH NI NADII HOW EAR FO THOSE IN INDIA WHO ARE OF HET THRNSIAIC TAHIF TECLERBAE THE CHRISTIAN FAITH CELEBRATE AITHMSSCR SA LELW. TYEH CHRISTMAS AS WELL. THEY OTREDECA HREIT HHCRUSCE IHWT DECORATE THEIR CHURCHES WITH A TBFLUEUIA WLFEOR ELALCD A BEAUTIFUL FLOWER CALLED HTE EITAPOSTIN NAD AGONM RO THE POINSETTIA AND MANGO OR BNAANA FSRFT RAF LLUFOYLRCO BANANA TREES ARE COLORFULLY RTDNONEMEA. ORNAMENTED

IN INDIA, C H A R I T Y IS CALLED, "BAKSHEESH."

121

FPTOORO ROOFTOP   OYJ JOY
TSNPEOAIIT POINSETTIA   DNAII INDIA
IASTELFV FESTIVAL   ISFTG GIFTS
NHDGTIMI MIDNIGHT   SAMS MASS
YRHACTI CHARITY   WLLA WALL
MIYFLA FAMILY   TPO POT

IN FINLAND, CHRISTMAS EVE, CHRISTMAS DAY, AND BOXING DAY ARE HELD TO BE THE THREE HOLY DAYS. CHRISTMAS DINNER IS CONSIDERED A FEAST AFTER A LIGHT BREAKFAST OF PLUM JUICE AND RICE PORRIDGE.

THE CHRISTMAS GREETING IN RUSSIA IS

"H R I S T O S RAZDAJETSJA."

THE COLLAPSE OF THE SOVIET UNION.

THE RUSSIAN PEOPLE ARE FREE TO CELEBRATE CHRISTMAS.

CHRISTMAS IN RUSSIA IS CELEBRATED FOR TWELVE DAYS, FROM DECEMBER 25 TO JANUARY 5.

RUSSIAN CELEBRATIONS INCLUDE CIRCUSES, SPORTS, AND CARNIVALS.

1. THIS LETTER BEGINS BOTH HEAR AND HERE.
   H
2. THIS LETTER ENDS BOTH BLOCK AND BLACK.
   K
3. THIS LETTER IS FOUND IN CAST BUT NOT IN LAST.
   C
4. IT ENDS THE WORD CAT AND BEGINS THE WORD TOY.
   T
5. IT APPEARS TWICE IN SOON AND ONCE IN HOT.
   O
6. IT'S FOUND ONCE IN FIVE AND TWICE IN VALVE.
   V
7. THIS LETTER IS FOUND IN GIFT BUT NOT IN RIFT.
   G
8. THIS LETTER BEGINS BOTH BLOCK AND BLACK.
   B

CHRISTIANS IN HONG KONG HAVE ADAPTED THE CHRISTMAS CELEBRATION INTO AN EASTERN SETTING. NATIVITY SCENES AND CHRISTMAS CARDS HAVE A CHINESE LOOK AND ARE VERY ARTISTIC.

I D E
O G R A P H
H O N G K O N G
S T R E A M E R S
C H I N E S E
C H A I N S
C H U R C H E S

J
F A N
J A P A N
O C T O P U S
J A P A N E S E
S L I P P E R S
F I S H

WEST   E(A)S(T)

WATER   L(A)(N)D

SHOES   S L (I) P P E R (S)

ADULT   (J) U V E N I L E

SOFT   H(A)R(D)

CAN YOU PRONOUNCE THE CHRISTMAS GEETING IN

(J)(A)(P)(A)(N): "SHINNEN

OMEDETO, KURISUMASU OMEDETO"? *WOW!*

D R W A R K Z V A J
J T X Z J W T P I X
L D V Y D G F S K H
Q M F X Q S (U) C T Y
E S W L C H R G E R
H P J I P Q A I (N) M
A V M M L X Y V M Q
K (B) C E W S F Z D S
G I K H E Z P Y R M
F G Y T C L (O) J H A

" B U O N NATALE" IS HOW YOU SAY MERRY
CHRISTMAS IN ITALY.

CHILDREN HOPE THAT "GESÙ BAMBINO" WILL BRING
THEM GIFTS. *WHO* IS HE?   BABY JESUS

"PRESEPIO" IS AN ITALIAN NAME FOR A FAMILIAR
CHRISTMAS SCENE. *WHAT* IS IT?   NATIVITY

THESE ARE SPECIAL "BAGS" THAT MEN MAKE
MUSIC ON. *WHAT* ARE THEY?
                                 BAGPIPES

IN ITALY, ONLY THIS MEAT IS EATEN ON THE FAST AT
CHRISTMAS EVE. *WHAT* IS IT?   FISH

NO ITALIAN MEAL CAN BE COMPLETE WITHOUT THIS
TRADITIONAL DISH. *WHAT* IS IT?   PASTA

MUSICIANS DRESS IN SHEEPSKIN JACKETS AS A
REMINDER OF THESE WHO WERE PRESENT AT
CHRIST'S BIRTH. *WHO* ARE THEY? SHEPHERDS

NI PINAS, THMSSCRIA EEV SI
IN SPAIN, CHRISTMAS EVE IS
OLAS ONWNK SA ETH GTNIH FO
A(L)SO KNOWN AS THE NIGHT OF
DOGO ITDIGNS. A IILNARDATTO
GOOD TIDINGS. A (T)RADITIONAL
MAGE SI EON HEWER DRIHCELN
GAME IS ONE WHE(R)E CHILDREN
HTI TA A RETE RNUKT LFLU
HIT AT A TRE(E) TRUNK FULL
FO IOODGSE, IRNGTY OT ONCKK
OF GOODIE(S), TRYING T(O) KNOCK
ETMH UTO.
THEM (O)UT.

SPAIN HAS A LEGEND OF A COAL MINER, NAMED

(O)(L)(E)(N)T z(E)(R)(O) WHO

CAME DOWN FROM A MOUNTAIN TO ANNOUNCE THE
BIRTH OF CHRIST.

138

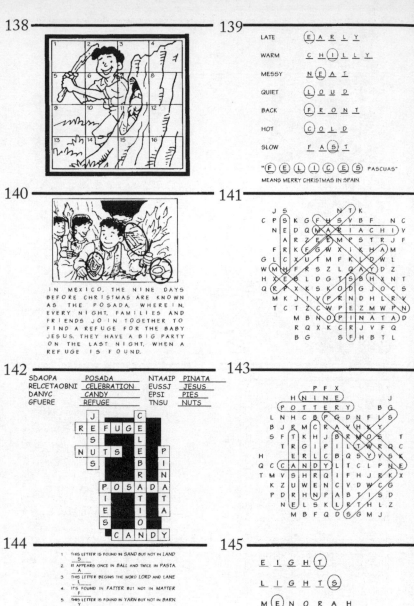

139

LATE	Ⓔ A R L Y
WARM	C H Ⓘ L L Y
MESSY	N Ⓔ A T
QUIET	Ⓛ O U D
BACK	Ⓕ R O N T
HOT	Ⓒ O L D
SLOW	F Ⓐ S T

"Ⓕ E L Ⓘ C Ⓔ Ⓢ PASCUAS"
MEANS MERRY CHRISTMAS IN SPAIN.

140

IN MEXICO, THE NINE DAYS BEFORE CHRISTMAS ARE KNOWN AS THE POSADA, WHERE IN EVERY NIGHT, FAMILIES AND FRIENDS JOIN TOGETHER TO FIND A REFUGE FOR THE BABY JESUS. THEY HAVE A BIG PARTY ON THE LAST NIGHT, WHEN A REFUGE IS FOUND.

141

(word search grid with MARIACHI, PINATA circled)

142

SDAOPA	POSADA	NTAAIP	PINATA
RELCETAOBNI	CELEBRATION	EUSSJ	JESUS
DANYC	CANDY	EPSI	PIES
GFUERE	REFUGE	TNSU	NUTS

(crossword grid)
REFUGE
NUTS
POSADA
CANDY

143

(word search grid with NINE, POTTERY, CANDY circled)

144

1. THIS LETTER IS FOUND IN SAND BUT NOT IN LAND
   S
2. IT APPEARS ONCE IN BALL AND TWICE IN PASTA.
   A
3. THIS LETTER BEGINS THE WORD LORD AND LANE
   L
4. IT'S FOUND IN FATTER BUT NOT IN MATTER
   F
5. THIS LETTER IS FOUND IN YARN BUT NOT IN BARN.
   Y

ALTHOUGH THEY DO NOT CELEBRATE CHRISTMAS IN ISRAEL, THEY DO HAVE AN IMPORTANT HOLIDAY AT THIS TIME OF THE YEAR. IT IS CALLED "HANUKKAH" AND IT IS ALSO KNOWN AS THE FESTIVAL OF LIGHTS AND IS REPRESENTED BY AN EIGHT-BRANCH MENORAH, OR CANDLE HOLDER. IT CELEBRATES A MIRACLE OF LONG AGO WHEN THE OIL, ONLY ENOUGH TO BURN FOR ONE DAY IN A LAMP, LASTED FOR EIGHT DAYS!

145

E I G H Ⓣ
L I G H T Ⓢ
M Ⓔ N O R A H
H A N U Ⓚ K A H
C H R I S T M Ⓐ S
H I S T O R I C A Ⓛ

POTATO PANCAKES OR Ⓛ Ⓐ Ⓣ Ⓚ Ⓔ Ⓢ
ARE A FAVORITE DISH AT HANUKKAH.

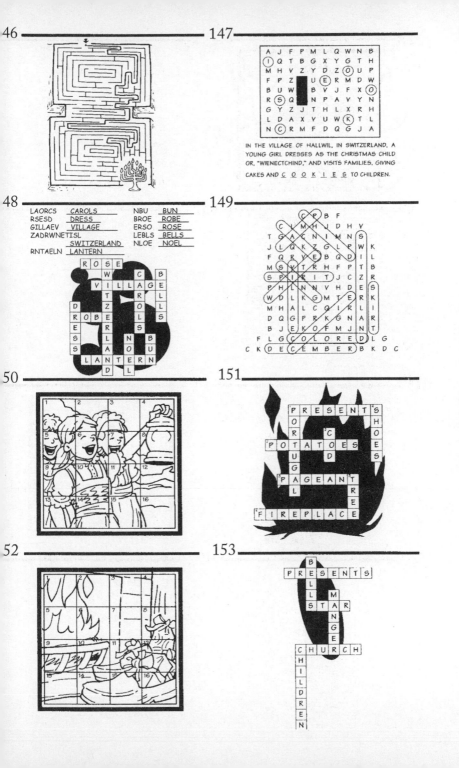

147

IN THE VILLAGE OF HALLWIL, IN SWITZERLAND, A YOUNG GIRL DRESSES AS THE CHRISTMAS CHILD OR, "WIENECTCHIND," AND VISITS FAMILIES, GIVING CAKES AND C O O K I E S TO CHILDREN.

48

LAORCS	CAROLS	NBU	BUN
RSESD	DRESS	BROE	ROBE
GILLAEV	VILLAGE	ERSO	ROSE
ZADRWNETISL		LEBLS	BELLS
	SWITZERLAND	NLOE	NOEL
RNTAELN	LANTERN		

149

50

151

52

153

HERE ARE THE
ANSWERS!

154

LNFAYI, HET AYD ADH VRREDIAI
FINALLY, (T)HE DAY HAD ARRIVED!
HOCL50 SWA OELDSC FRO ETH
SCHOOL WA(S) CLOSED FO(R) THE
AIOLDSYH NAD LAL HTE SDKI
HOL(I)DAYS AND ALL T(H)E KIDS
ERHSUD UTO, EAERG OFR HTAW
RU(S)HED OUT, EAGER FOR WHAT
AWS HDAEA. THMSASCRI ASW
WAS AHEAD. (C)HRISTMAS WAS
NOMGCI DAN HOW UWPLTON' EB
COMING AND WHO WOULDN'T BE
DECXTEI BTAUO ATTH?
EXCITED (A)BOUT THAT ?

ITLL BE
(C)(H)(R)(I)(S)(T)(M)(A)(S) SOON!

155

SCHO OL'S O̲U̲T FOR CHRIST-
MAS A̲N̲D THE HOL̲I̲DAYS
HAVE BEGU̲N̲!

157

SI̲L̲E̲N̲T̲ NI̲ G̲H̲T̲. HO̲L̲Y̲
N̲I̲G̲H̲T̲.

C̲ H̲R̲I̲S̲T̲M̲A̲S̲ T̲R̲E̲E̲.

C̲ H̲R̲I̲S̲T̲M̲A̲S̲ S̲T̲O̲C̲K̲I̲N̲G̲S̲.

L̲I̲T̲T̲L̲E̲ T̲O̲W̲N̲ O̲F̲
B̲E̲T̲H̲L̲E̲H̲E̲M̲.

J̲E̲S̲U̲S̲ I̲S̲ B̲O̲R̲N̲.

T̲H̲E̲ T̲W̲E̲L̲V̲E̲ D̲A̲Y̲S̲ O̲F̲
C̲H̲R̲I̲S̲T̲M̲A̲S̲.

160

161

162

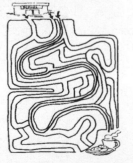

163

G O (D)
P L A (Y)
S P (O) O N
S C H O (O) L
S N O W (M) (A) N
S (H) (E) P H E R D
C H R I S T M A S
I N S (T) (R) U C T O (R)

ENJOY THE
(H)(O)(L)(I)(D)(A)(Y)(S)

THIS MAN HAS A LOT TO TEACH YOU IF YOU SHOW UP ONCE A WEEK. *WHO* IS HE? PASTOR

HE'LL SHOW YOU HOW TO GET DOWN THE MOUNTAIN SAFELY. *WHO* IS HE? SKI INSTRUCTOR

IT DOESN'T FLY AND IT MAKES YOUR MOUTH WATER EVERY YEAR. *WHAT* IS IT? TURKEY

IT IS VERY DIFFICULT WAITING TO FIND OUT THE CONTENTS OF THIS. *WHAT* IS IT? GIFT

AT THIS TIME OF YEAR, YOU'RE THINKING OF WHAT IS AHEAD. *WHERE* ARE YOU? SCHOOL

D	J	F	O	A	M	B	L	Q	U
C	I	X	P	S	Y	P	G	N	E
K	M	R	N	K	E	B	V	W	X
G	P	S	W	D	■	■	Q	C	J
N	L	Q	O	B	T	F	W	N	D
F	A	Y	I	G	C	S	I	M	V
O	C	X	K	Y	P	J	L	A	K
J	W	H	V	E	Y	X	O	V	Q
A	E	S	I	M	L	B	G	D	F

SNOWBALL FIGHTS ARE A LOT OF FUN, BUT TRY NOT TO H U R T ANYONE!

Crossword puzzle (67): CHRISTMAS, CONCERTS, SP, FORT, PR, STR, LOG, CART, CRI, SNOWBOARD, JESUS, ICE

ERTE — TREE
KURTYE — TURKEY
ENRTANSOM — ORNAMENTS
NSRTEPF — PRESENT
HHBFTELME — BETHLEHEM
IANSGTK — SKATING

Crossword puzzle (168): SKIING, PRESENT, BETHLEHEM, ORNAMENTS, TURKEY, TREE

1. BEGINS THE WORD NUT AND ENDS THE WORD MOON. N
2. APPEARS ONCE IN ICE AND TWICE IN SKIIS. I
3. THIS LETTER IS FOUND IN BEGAN BUT NOT IN BEGUN. A
4. APPEARS TWICE IN BOOT BUT ONLY ONCE IN POLE. O
5. FOUND TWICE IN BOTH SNOWSHOE AND SOCKS. S
6. YOU'LL FIND THIS IN LESS BUT NOT IN LOSS. E
7. BEGINS TREE AND IS IN THE MIDDLE OF MOTOR. T
8. APPEARS ONCE IN SISTER AND TWICE IN BROTHER. R

"YOU WILL BE WITH CHILD AND GIVE BIRTH TO A SON, AND YOU ARE TO GIVE HIM THE NAME JESUS"

SNOW	R A I N
UP	D O W N
RECEIVE	G I V E
DARK	L I G H T
FULL	E M P T Y
HAPPY	S A D
SISTER	B R O T H E R

CHRIST, THE TRUE
M E A N I N G
OF CHRISTMAS.

ON NLBAOLWS GTIHF SI EOPMLETC
NO SNOWBALL FIGHT IS COMPLETE

HTUTOIW A NRFWOOTS OT RERTATE
WITHOUT A SNOWFORT TO RETREAT

OT DAN EIHD NI. KMAE SA YANM
TO AND HIDE IN. MAKE AS MANY

OSWN CRKISB SA DENEDE DAN
SNOW BRICKS AS NEEDED AND

TCAKS HMTE NO AHEC ORHET, KIGANM
STACK THEM ON EACH OTHER, MAKING

SREU HET ITNSOJREA GGDTSREAE.
SURE THE JOINTS ARE STAGGERED.

U'YLOL EB BVNCEIINL!
YOU'LL BE INVINCIBLE!

YOU'LL NEED A
S N O W F O R T

THE THREE WISE MEN.

TURKEY WITH ALL THE TRIMMINGS.

CHRIST, THE SAVIOR, IS BORN.

IT'S BETTER TO GIVE THAN TO RECEIVE.

CHRISTMAS EVE.

MERRY CHRISTMAS AND A HAPPY NEW YEAR!

176

T O B O G G A N

S N O W F O R T

S N O W M O B I L E

I C E F I S H I N G

D R U M

S N O W M A N

WHAT'S REALLY, REALLY BIG AND COVERED WITH SNOW?

M O U N T A I N

177

SKIS HELP GET YOU QUICKLY FROM THE TOP TO THE BOTTOM. *WHERE* ARE YOU? **MOUNTAIN**

THIS PERSON RECEIVED A MIRACLE AND THE SAVIOR WAS BORN . *WHO* WAS IT? **MARY**

THREE MEN FROM THE EAST VISITED THIS SMALL TOWN. *WHERE* WERE THEY? **BETHLEHEM**

IT IS MADE WAY UP NORTH, BUT YOU CAN MAKE ONE TOO. *WHAT* IS IT? **IGLOO**

WITH THIS AND A HORSE YOU CAN GO ANYWHERE IN THE SNOW. *WHAT* IS IT? **SLEIGH**

ON THIS, YOU ENJOY THE SAME SPORT IN WINTER AND SUMMER. *WHAT* ARE THEY? **SKIS**

178

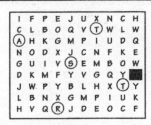

179

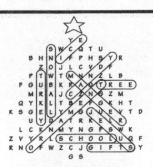

180

CHRISTMAS IS A TIME TO S T A R T THINKING ABOUT OTHERS!

181

S K I

G I V E

I G L O O

D I N N E R

P R E S E N T

H O L I D A Y S

B E T H L E H E M

"TO YOU, A S A V I O R IS BORN."

84

S N O W S H O E S (crossword)
G L O V E S
S N O W M A N
B A S K E T
S N O W M O B I L E
S K I S

185

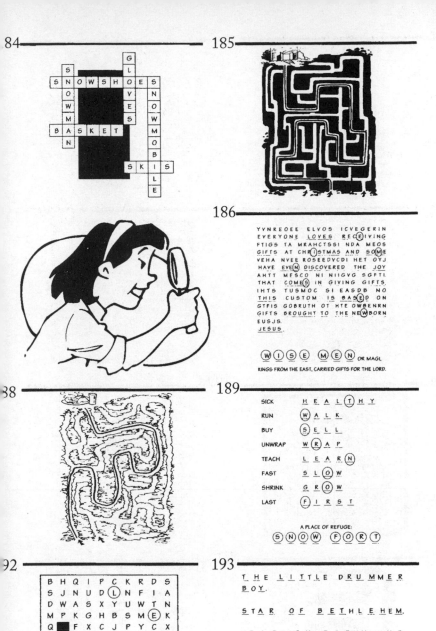

186

YVNREOEE ELVOS ICVEGERIN
EVERYONE LOVES RECEIVING
FTIGS TA MRAHCTSSI NDA MEOS
GIFTS AT CHRISTMAS AND SOME
VEHA NVEE ROSEEDYCDI HET OYJ
HAVE EVEN DISCOVERED THE JOY
AHTT MESCO NI NIIGVG SGFTI
THAT COMES IN GIVING GIFTS.
IHTS TUSMOC SI EASDB NO
THIS CUSTOM IS BASED ON
GTFIS GOBRUTH OT HTE OWBENRN
GIFTS BROUGHT TO THE NEWBORN
EUSJS.
JESUS.

WISE MEN OR MAGI,
KINGS FROM THE EAST, CARRIED GIFTS FOR THE LORD.

188

189

SICK — HEALTHY
RUN — WALK
BUY — SELL
UNWRAP — WRAP
TEACH — LEARN
FAST — SLOW
SHRINK — GROW
LAST — FIRST

A PLACE OF REFUGE: SNOW FORT

192

B H Q I P C K R D S
S J N U D L N F I A
D W A S X Y U W T N
M P K G H B S M E K
Q ■ F X C J P Y C X
C Q N Y T G H W Q
G U M X F W A R J B
R A T J U I P Y V R
M O I G H B T D F K

JESUS WAS BORN BECAUSE OF GOD'S LOVE FOR YOU! IN HIM, YOU TOO CAN L O V E OTHERS.

193

THE LITTLE DRUMMER BOY.

STAR OF BETHLEHEM.

PEACE ON EARTH AND GOOD WILL TO MEN.

A BABY LYING IN A MANGER.

WHITE CHRISTMAS.

194

1. IT CAN BE FOUND IN *LAST* BUT NOT IN *LOST*.
   A
2. LOOK FOR IT ONCE IN BOTH *TOY* AND IN *YELL*.
   Y
3. THIRD IN PLACE IN BOTH *RENT* AND IN *LENT*.
   N
4. IT CAN BE FOUND IN *SONG* BUT NOT IN *SANG*.
   O
5. IT DOUBLES BOTH *BOOTS* AND *TOBOGANS*.
   S
6. THIS LETTER BEGINS *ROUND* AND ENDS *HOUR*.
   R
7. IT IS FOUND AT THE BEGINNING OF *JAM* AND *JOY*.
   J

"WHE<u>N</u> THE<u>Y</u> <u>S</u>A<u>W</u> THE <u>S</u>T<u>A</u><u>R</u>,
   3   2   5 1 4   5 1 6
THE<u>Y</u> WERE <u>O</u>VER<u>J</u>O<u>Y</u>ED. <u>O</u>N
   2   4   7 1 2   4 5
<u>C</u>O<u>M</u>IN<u>G</u> <u>T</u>O THE HO<u>U</u>SE, THEY
 6   1   4   5 5   5
<u>S</u> <u>A</u>W THE CHILD WITH HI<u>S</u> <u>M</u>OTHER
 5   1   5   1
MAR<u>Y</u>, <u>A</u>ND THEY BO<u>W</u>ED DO<u>W</u>N
      2   1   6 5   2   4 3
<u>A</u>ND WOR<u>S</u>HIPED HIM."
 1 3   4 6 5

MATTHEW 2:10-11

195

```
          R J K M Y K S Q H W T Y
  T R Z M T L T G W K O H F H O
 (B E L L S)O D L I Z B L Z O L
  H W E Q H K U Y U N G L A H I
  Q M S L U P F N H L S Y H D A
  K G I B F K G L T T L E W A Y
  D Z L S Q T V J R A Q T L A
  K T E D K H A E T W I R B J
 (C A N D L E)C P E V K N U W
  E B T Q F N K Z R F Q D G L
  L W U Y O G W M S L B N Q T
  M P F C E J L W F T P G Y P
  S G             (T O Y S)
```

196

```
              H O L L Y
  P R E S E N T
                T R E E
  O R N A M E N T
              W R E A T H
  S N O W B A L L
  T U R K E Y
  B E T H L E H E M
```
LITTLE TOWN OF DAVID.

197

MIRHSTCAS SI OS CMHU FNU
CHRISTMAS IS <u>SO</u> MUCH FUN
NAD EYRVE ERYA VAEESL IGSTNAL
AND EVERY YEAR LEAVES LASTING
ERSIMMOE. PGEINKE NI DIMN OT
MEMORIES. KEEPING IN MIND TO
EB NCOTREAIEDS OT OTESH
BE CONSIDERATE TO THOSE
NRAODU OYU SALVEE UYO HWTI
AROUND YOU LEAVES YOU WITH
MMOEESIR FO A RVYE ICPEASL
MEMORIES OF A VERY SPECIAL
IDKN.
KIND.

A BLESSED CHRISTMAS IS IN BEING KIND TO
O T H E R S

198

199

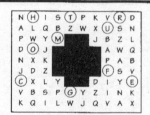

THE WINTER SEASON IS FULL OF M U C H FUN
AND EXCITEMENT, BUT DON'T F O R G E T
WHAT IT'S REALLY ABOUT.

202

THANKS FOR PLAYING!